Critical Leadership and Management Tools for Contemporary Organizations

Critical Leadership and Management Tools for Contemporary Organizations

Dr. Tony Miller

BEP
BUSINESS EXPERT PRESS
Leader in applied, concise business books

Critical Leadership and Management Tools for Contemporary Organizations

First published in 2023 by
Business Expert Press, LLC
222 East 46th Street, New York, NY 10017
www.businessexpertpress.com

ISBN-13: 978-1-63742-520-6 (paperback)
ISBN-13: 978-1-63742-521-3 (e-book)

Business Expert Press Human Resource Management and Organizational Behavior Collection

First edition: 2023

10 9 8 7 6 5 4 3 2 1

Description

A massive paradigm shift in the world of work **and** the way we manage people. What's changing—everything!

All of this has been brought about by several converging factors. The impact of COVID-19 on how we work; causing a shift from where work is done. Recent significant changes in artificial intelligence, ChatGPT, and robotics will impact on every area of work worldwide—it's happening now.

Predictably, fewer people are now required in the world of work; those with a potentially amazing career will be talented people who will be paid on what they do rather than what they know—a huge change.

A new type of management. Inspirational leaders with a special skillset will be in high demand. Managers of the past are unlikely to have the skills or personality to get the best from the new breed of super employees.

In this book, we will look at all these issues and provide readers with the current facts, case studies from the world's leading companies, worked examples, and most importantly, practical advice on *how to do it*.

Keywords

algorithms; analysis skills; appraisal; artificial intelligence; automation; bonus; change; cognitive learning; compensation; competence; differentiation; deep learning; employee motivation; employment trends; generation Z; home working; human resources; hybrid working; iGen; inspirational leadership; key leadership skills; leadership; leadership style; managers; management; motivation; OCEAN; organizational design (OD); performance appraisal; personality; poor performers; productivity; profiling; reliability; remote working; rewards right sizing; robotics; paradigm shifts; talented employees

Contents

CHAPTER 1

A Paradigm Shift in the Way We Manage People

The End of the Manager?

You do not need to be a genius to notice the massive change in the world of work. Massive change on a scale unimaginable due to robotic technology, artificial intelligence (AI), and the impact of COVID-19 changing where we work.

One of the most significant changes in organizational terms from a people perspective is that of the future of the manager. With so much change and the advent of home working on a massive scale, what are the manager's functions and purpose in today's world of unprecedented rapid change? In a recent report by Goldman Sachs, the forecast was that *Management* 32 percent would be directly affected by AI (March 2023).

Does the world's most highly educated workforce need managing as they were in years gone by? Indeed, the post of a manager has been in decline for years. Top companies phased out managers, and most of the world's top 10 wealthiest companies have leaders, not managers. Therefore, the future will be managed by a new breed—the inspirational leader, someone who can commit to the future and works by guidelines rather than a rule book of instructions. The available data show that this works and produces better productivity and lower staff turnover. It's inevitable that rules and regulations will be governed in future by AI.

The difference between leaders and managers?

More about managers. Courtis, in a book entitled *Managed by Mistake*, which looked at sad management, noted that "basic and essential management principles are being flouted everywhere…." Mistakes made by managers fall crudely into five categories:

1. *Errors of omission* (failure to act or communicate)
2. *Errors of commission* (doing things you ought not to have done)

3. *Qualitative errors* (doing the right thing inadequately or by the wrong method)
4. *Errors of timing* (doing the right thing too early or too late)
5. *Credibility errors* (doing the right thing, at the right time, but in such a way as to irritate everyone or discredit the action)

The corporate oversight of many board directors would be unnecessary if managers were doing their jobs correctly. Managers can be classified into three groups, sad, mad, and bad.

The specific problem is that managerial incompetence causes employee stress, leading to illness and absenteeism, which in turn leads to more significant costs to the company. Vicious circles like this are a function of managerial competence levels.

While sad managers are the result of bad appointments, *mad* managers are the real focus. They are not mad in the ordinary sense but near madness or subclinical pathology. This makes them both attractive and successful at times but ultimately leads to their derailment. Their dark side, usually well under control, comes out in terms of stress and derails them.

Sad, incompetent managers are too easy to spot. Often they do not have what it takes to rise up the organization. It is bad and mad managers, often who are both, that are the real derailers. Bad managers—bullies, despots, tyrants—thrive in times of chaos, flux, or uncertainty. Their toxicity and wickedness may quickly become apparent.

A manager fills the requirement of a job. New Leadership is more a way of life with a strong focus on the future and the development of others. TM 1..2023

Can managers be transformed into leaders (see Figure 1.1)?

It is a difficult question, and training providers will tell you they can do it. The truth is it depends on the person's personality and willingness to make a significant and irrevocable change. As we know, personality is difficult, if not impossible, to change. It is therefore very important for the leader to have the appropriate personality and attitude from the start and the ability to assemble the right skillset (see Figure 1.2).

Difference between leaders and managers—a quick view

1. Leaders create a vision, managers create goals
2. Leaders are change agents, managers maintain the status quo
3. Leaders are unique, managers copy
4. Leaders take risks, managers control risk
5. Leaders are in it for the long haul, managers think short-term
6. Leaders grow personally, managers rely on existing, proven skills
7. Leaders build relationships, managers build systems and processes
8. Leaders coach, managers direct
9. Leaders create fans, managers have employees

Figure 1.1 *Difference between leaders and managers*

Credit: William Arruda is the cofounder of CareerBlast as published in Forbes.

To explain better, we need to look at the personality most likely to succeed in a leadership role in an organizational environment. The most chosen personality profiler today is the McCrae and Costa five-factor model. This model has become the benchmark and is used in the big AI compilation of Facebook personality data.

You can use an online questionnaire or paper-and-pencil questionnaire to determine the person's profile. It can be done using the version NEO-PI-3, which shows the Big Five; OCEAN.

OCEAN has become the industry gold standard, or NEO as it is referred to in Europe. The more extensive version of this is Personality Inventory, Revised edition (NEO-PI-R).

AI profile information has also been gathered. It is available from organizations such as Cambridge University in the UK and Stanford University in California using data collected from Facebook likes. This may be available from Facebook Direct.

The preferred personality profile has become the Big Five OCEAN, much of the data looking at Personality is by AI. A short historical explanation follows.

Costa and McCrae's Big Five

Costa and McCrae revived the world of personality theory and testing. Working within the psychometric trait tradition, they settled on three and then five dimensions of personality. Now called the *five-factor*

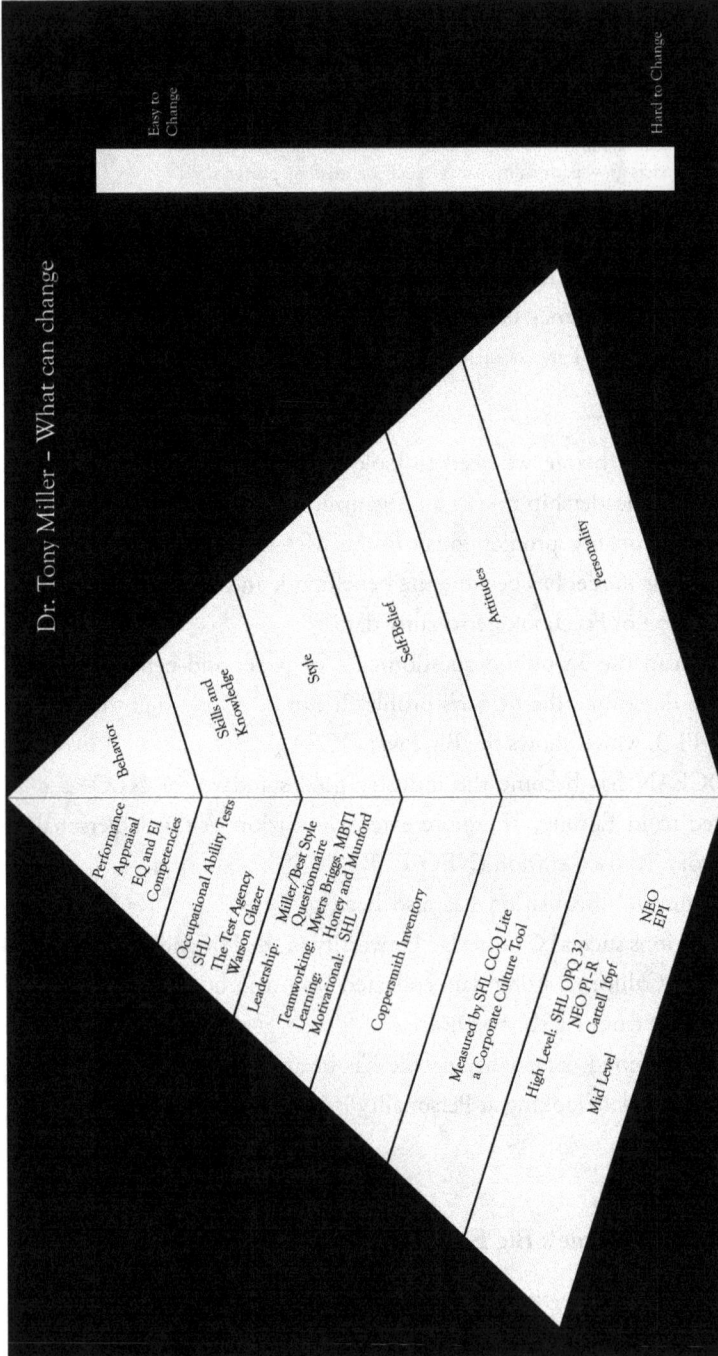

Figure 1.2 What we can change

OCEAN

Openness   Conscientiousness   Extroversion   Agreeableness   Neuroticism

High

Mid

Low

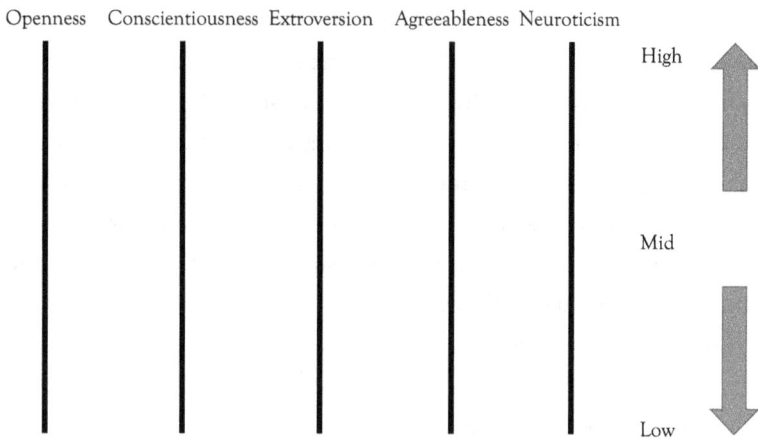

Figure 1.3 Profile chart of the Big Five

approach (FFA) or *five-factor model* (FFM) (see Figure 1.3). It is more commonly called OCEAN—as it is an acronym for the five factors. There is now broad agreement on the approach/model, which seems to be the profile adopted by AI. Also included are those who adopt the lexical approach—those who look at natural language and the relationship between everyday terms for personality traits (Goldberg). Indeed, there is an active psycho-lexical tradition in the personality theory that attempts to *recover* the basic dimensions of personality through analysis of natural language. Researchers have found impressive evidence, across various languages, of the emergence of similar factors, which are analogous to the *Big Five*. However, they have not looked at the association between personality traits and work outcomes. There are vigorous critiques of the FFM, but these have not reduced its popularity among personality researchers. Block, Eysenck, and Costa and McCrae argue that there are five basic unrelated dimensions of personality.

Can Artificial Intelligence Tell Us Someone's Personality?

How accurate is it? Can an AI algorithm really tell someone's personality? Michal Kosinski, Associate Professor in Organizational Behavior at Stanford University Graduate School of Business, has done numerous presentations on this. He states why and how an algorithm can out predict your personality compared to a human. Eleven Facebook likes will be more accurate than a work colleague. "The most accurate of the judges; your spouse can be beaten by 250 likes" on Facebook. This is using the OCEAN model, and of course, this algorithm, computer-generated profiling, is of immense use to employers when recruiting and when making decisions on future leaders or for those suitable for remote working. This information has already been gathered, so there is no questionnaire to complete; it is just a download.

The five personality traits measured are as follows:

1. The first observable trait in the OCEAN personality traits model is *openness* to experience, which describes an individual's creativity, curiosity, and culture. Openness to experience explores an individual's willingness to try new things and ability to think outside the box when tasked with something difficult. High scores are described as curious, creative, imaginative, and unconventional. Participants with a low score are considered more predictable and resistant to change.

High	Average	Low
Open to new experiences. You have broad interests and are very imaginative.	Practical but willing to consider new ways of doing things. You seek a balance between the old and the new.	Down-to-earth, practical, traditional, and pretty much set in your ways.

2. The personality trait of *conscientiousness* relates to an individual's hardworking nature, organization, and dependability. Individuals with a high conscientiousness rating have high competence, good organization, strong self-discipline, and a drive to obtain recognition or achievement. Those high in this score make very reliable home workers.

High	Average	Low
Conscientious and well-organized. You have high standards and always strive to achieve your goals.	Dependable and moderately well-organized. You generally have clear goals but are able to set your work aside.	Easygoing, not very well-organized, and sometimes careless. You prefer not to make plans.

3. *Extraversion* is the personality trait used to comment on an individual's sociability, assertiveness, and outgoing nature toward others. It can be measured by observing an individual's energy during and after social interaction and confidence while speaking to others. Low scores on the scale are known as introverts.

High	Average	Low
Extraverted, outgoing, active, and high-spirited. You prefer to be around people most of the time.	Moderate in activity and enthusiasm. You enjoy the company of others, but you also value privacy.	Introverted, reserved, and serious. You prefer to be alone or with a few close friends.

4. *Agreeableness* refers to how people tend to treat relationships with others. Unlike extraversion, which consists of pursuing relationships, agreeableness focuses on people's orientation and interactions with others. Those low in agreeableness may be perceived as suspicious, manipulative, and uncooperative.

High	Average	Low
Compassionate, good-natured, and eager to cooperate and avoid conflict.	Generally warm, trusting, and agreeable, but you can sometimes be stubborn and competitive.	Hard-headed, skeptical, proud, and competitive. You tend to express your anger directly.

5. **Neuroticism**

   Those who score high on neuroticism often feel anxious, insecure, and self-pitying. They are often perceived as moody and irritable. They are prone to excessive sadness and low self-esteem.

High	Average	Low
Sensitive, emotional, and prone to experience feelings that are upsetting.	Generally calm and able to deal with stress, but you sometimes experience feelings of guilt, anger, or sadness.	Secured, hardy, and generally relaxed even under stressful conditions.

The personality likely to make a good leader (depending on the organization and world location) is likely to be:

O. High openness to deliver change and future needs

C. High conscientiousness: needed for the drive to be persistent and resolute in goals and change needed in the future

E. Relatively high as there will often be a significant need to persuade others and be a master of communication

A. Agreeableness, midrange, and higher

N. Neuroticism on the low side; the new leader with be a stressful and very observed post

The Leader and What Is Needed

Many books on leadership share rip-roaring stories based on the military, sports celebrities, and those who put together exciting stories that are better confined to amusing fiction. This book is about the world of work and what does or does not work with practical, how-to-do-it examples.

We have looked at the likely personality traits needed for a good leader, which should be invaluable for those in the organization responsible for hiring.

When looking at the skill set for a leader in today's business world, there are six skills that need to be mastered and delivered daily. You could rank yourself on each of the skills and devise a program to help you to improve your individual skills if needed.

> The leadership and key traits make the leadership for the future completely bias-free.
>
> The personality profile is key. Decisions can then be free from bias such as age, race, gender, religion, or ethnic background.

The six skills are not in any ranked order and are as follows:

Leadership skill 1; leadership is about committing to something that has not yet happened.

The role of the leader is to be in the present but always looking to the future. The leader must always be one step ahead. Being relaxed with the present and living mentally in the past is very comfortable; that is a manager. Being future-focused requires a lot of bravery, an open mind, and acceptance of the significant change. In our current world, in the last two years, we have seen more change and innovation than at any time of humankind's history—that's a fact.

Leadership skills 2; power and responsibility. The two come together, and with that comes absolute accountability.

"The buck stops here" is a saying that good leaders understand and live with. The leadership role requires a high level of honesty and integrity. These need to be demonstrated daily to establish trust and respect.

Leaders are respected for their actions—not because they hold a job title.

Leaders listen carefully and speak softly to other employees, all while being respectful. They rely on earning dependability of their constituents. They will also acknowledge their own fault whenever necessary.
                                                              —2022, Jeff Bezos, Amazon

Leadership skill 3; the leader must have a process to set, measure, and reward objectives to get the best consistent results.

This is very difficult to do as some of the processes (pay and bonuses) are controlled by others. Also, performance appraisal is supposed to be the most important goal-setting process but rarely is any effort made to measure its cost-effectiveness or contribution to improving motivation and productivity.

Methods of improving appraisal, pay and bonus and setting objectives are covered in future chapters and are essential for leaders to master.

Leadership skill 4; great leaders recognize that communication takes time, and that you cannot correct the past.

Communicate constantly—especially to your team. You cannot expect total commitment if your team does not know what is happening. This is critically important. People are individuals; during a time of change, such as we are experiencing now; they move through the process at different speeds—some requiring more time and clarification than others. In personality terms, low 0s will always be difficult.

The four stages of individual change are as follows (see Figure 1.4).

Negation

- It won't work.
- What a stupid idea.

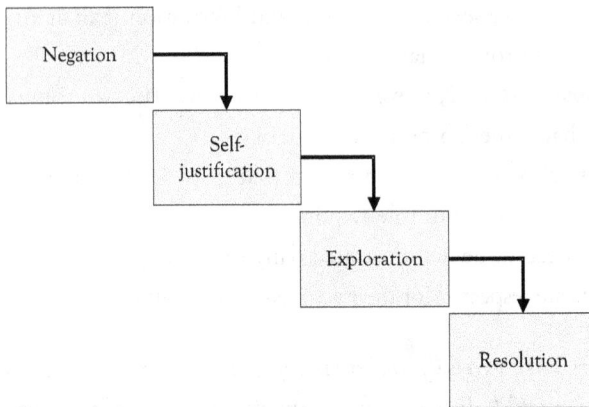

Figure 1.4 Four stages of individual change

- We have tried this before.
- It cannot be done.

Self-Justification

- I do not have the skills or knowledge to do this.
- I'm too old to change my ways.
- It's' all happening too quickly.
- I just do not understand.

Exploration

- Can I get more information?
- Will I get training?
- Will there be a Q&A session?
- What is the timeline?

Resolution

- I would like to be involved in the implementation team.
- When will my training/orientation take place?
- Why can't we do this sooner?
- We should have done this years ago.

Leadership skill 5; it is the leader's job to make sure people know what is going on.

Most teams or departments are almost in silos—they are not in a position to see the big picture—the leader is the only one who has this unique advantage. This applies to the broader group, not just your team. Use every communication channel open to you.

Leadership skill 6; bring out the best in *everyone.*

Help others to be the best they can be. Focus on what they have done well. Often old-style managers spend too much time chastising people for what they have done wrong rather than praising them for when they have done a great job. A helpful leadership maxim to remember is "Success breeds success."

Bring out the best in everyone, and everyone is a winner:

When you give everyone a voice and give people power, the system usually ends up in a really good place. So, what we view our role as, is giving people that power.

—Mark Zuckerburg, Facebook

Great business leaders today have the ability and discipline to be future-focused. They are prepared to take risks and have the persistence and drive to see things through despite adversity. They also have the skill to get people around them that can transform ideas into action. Some of the best examples are in the IT world, Microsoft, Google, Facebook, and Apple, to name but a few.

Then there is Tesla; who would ever have thought that in just a few years, a maker of electric cars would become a world leader? Due to the foresight, persistence, and vision of Elon Musk.

Tools That Will Help Develop Leaders

The marketplace is full of good advice for budding leaders; personality is crucial and also a few well-chosen tools that can be used, particularly when helping people to become influential leaders.

It is time to invest in yourself. If you want to be the leader of the future, perhaps it's time to invest in yourself. This comment was very well put by Warren Buffett, one of the greatest financial investors of our time.

"The best investment you can make, is an investment in yourself. The more you learn, the more you will earn."

Here are two tools you may find of use; the first is to identify your leadership style. The second is to show how you allocate your time.

Our first tool is a self-reporting questionnaire designed to show where your current approach is on a leadership style grid. In the words of *Henry A. Kissinger*, who made the very wise comment:

> "If you do not know where you are going, every road will get you nowhere."

Identify Your Leadership Style

Introduction

- This questionnaire is designed to help evaluate aspects of your leadership style.
- You will be asked to comment on how you approach work by considering the strength of capability with regard to certain behaviors or the frequency with which these behaviors are displayed.
- The object is to identify your current style.
- You should therefore respond as honestly and as quickly as possible.

Guidelines

- Allocate points to each statement, be honest and score yourself on how you are or act now.
- Details of the scoring are given at the top of each section.
- Score all of the questions.

Response Sheet

- After completing the questions, fill in the response score sheet. You will see that your score is entered in the box next to the appropriate question number.

- When you have completed the page—total the columns vertically, adding up the scores you have just completed.
- The total of the scores in columns with odd-numbered questions gives you the score for Leadership style – the total of columns (A + C).
- The total of the scores in columns with even-numbered questions gives you the score for Task focus (B + D).
- The other gives you the key to change the number you have for LEADERSHIP (A + C) to a chart number—plot this on the chart. Then change the number you have for TASK (B + D) again, convert them, and record them.
- You will now see your task and leadership style.

Section 1

This section deals with perceived ability at performing in a certain way; answer from your perception as to how effective you are at these activities if completing the questionnaire for yourself.

For each of the following statements, decide which of the answers on the following scale best applies and score accordingly:

| 5 | Very strong in this area

| 4 | Some strengths in this area

| 3 | Capable in this area

| 2 | Occasionally ineffective in this area

| 1 | Clear development needs in this area

1. Listening to others without being critical
2. Focusing single-mindedly on what needs to be done
3. Holding back when others may be about to do tasks in their way
4. Directing effort toward priorities and end goals
5. Inviting comments on own ideas
6. Maintaining a quality focus on tasks
7. Consulting on issues where input decisions will be taken
8. Monitoring performance against targets
9. Defining broad areas for achievement without specifying detailed methods
10. Delivering against stretching targets

For each of the following statements, decide which of the answers on the following scale best applies and score accordingly:

| 5 | Very strong in this area | | 2 | Occasionally ineffective in this area |

| 4 | Some strengths in this area | | 1 | Clear development needs in this area |

| 3 | Capable in this area |

11. Keeping others informed of developments that may affect them
12. Measuring outputs to gauge performance
13. Involving others fully in the workings of the area
14. Running an efficient operation
15. Allowing others to plan their own work
16. Delivering consistently high level of results
17. Letting go of decision-making power
18. Managing resources effectively
19. Encouraging others to implement their ideas
20. Improving work practices

Section 2

This section deals with how often a certain style of operating is evidenced.

For each of the following statements, decide which of the answers on the following scale best applies and score accordingly:

| 5 | Happens most of the time | | 2 | Happens occasionally |

| 4 | Happens often | | 1 | Happens rarely |

| 3 | Happens sometimes |

1. Consulting with own team about forthcoming decisions
2. Highlighting the need to achieve results
3. Staying silent when in disagreement with own staff's decisions
4. Raising quality standards on tasks
5. Finding necessary resources to support the team's initiatives
6. Identifying clear priorities in work
7. Setting a broad goal that others can meet in their own way
8. Setting deadlines for task completion
9. Asking for ideas prior to tackling tasks
10. Reviewing achievements against objectives
11. Leaving it to the group to organize their activities
12. Defining what needs to be achieved on tasks
13. Supporting team decisions against opposition
14. Devising plans and concrete objectives for others
15. Involving individuals in drawing up plans
16. Setting clear objectives and goals for activities
17. Coaching others without giving direct advice
18. Scheduling activities for completion
19. Incorporating others' ideas into own plans
20. Focusing effort solely on key tasks

Response Score Sheet

Enter your response score to each question in the relevant box.

Section One

1 ☐	2 ☐	3 ☐	4 ☐
5 ☐	6 ☐	7 ☐	8 ☐
9 ☐	10 ☐	11 ☐	12 ☐
13 ☐	14 ☐	15 ☐	16 ☐
17 ☐	18 ☐	19 ☐	20 ☐

Section Two

1 ☐	2 ☐	3 ☐	4 ☐
5 ☐	6 ☐	7 ☐	8 ☐
9 ☐	10 ☐	11 ☐	12 ☐
13 ☐	14 ☐	15 ☐	16 ☐
17 ☐	18 ☐	19 ☐	20 ☐

A =   B =   C =   D=

A + C = Leadership style …..   B + D = task focus…….

Style
Questionnaire
Marking Guide

TOTAL SCORE	1–10 ON GRID
96 and above	10
92 and above	9
88 and above	8
84 and above	7
80 and above	6
76 and above	5
72 and above	4
68 and above	3
64 and above	2
60 and above	1

Leadership Style Questionnaire

The grid shows your balance of leadership styles.

	1	2	3	4	5	6	7	8	9	10
High 10										
9										
8										
7										
6										
TASK 5										
4										
3										
2										
Low 1										

	1	2	3	4	5	6	7	8	9	10

Directive   **Delegative**   **Consultative**   **Participative**

Leadership Style

About Leadership Style

Leadership style has changed dramatically in the last few years. Better employees, global competition, and e-business have all had a dramatic effect on how we manage and lead our employees.

The leadership styles are the Bass and Stogdill labels used for clarity and standardization. With the rapidly increasing use of teams, it's clear that the appropriate leadership style is critical if a radical improvement in performance is needed. The styles also link conveniently with the Tuckman stages of team development and the four types of working teams.

Leadership Labels

Directive, this is the real authoritarian way of managing, *I tell—you do.* Its use is a real problem in today's business world. It assumes that you are leading stupid people—who can't be trusted. People using this style are the least flexible and the hardest to change. However, it's still the predominant style in many regions of the world.

Delegative, a more flexible style, suitable for the first two stages of the Tuckman team development model—forming and storming. This type will work for teams but *not* empowered teams if the best results are sought. This style has been a lifelong favorite of Warren Buffett, arguably the world's most successful investor.

Consultative, this style is a good style for newly empowered teams that seek some guidance and help—it is also appropriate at the Tuckman *norming stage*. Realistically, this is as flexible as most leaders and organizations get to lead teams. Empowered teams are working at a 1:50 ratio.

Participative, the style for high ratio empowered teams and self-managing teams. This style requires true leadership skills as defined for today. It is a style that will get the most from the teams and give the greatest flexibility. Leaders with this style tend to get the best results, particularly from talented people, and can easily switch to other leadership styles when circumstances require it—used to great effect by most of the world's richest companies and also by Richard Branson, creator of Virgin Atlantic and Virgin Music.

Dr. Tony Miller and Bill Best 2023.

The Adair Model

Another helpful tool focuses on how you spend your time as a leader. It shows clearly if you are a people-focused leader or if you a simply task-focused. Successful leaders are well-rounded and are able to use the balance of people and tasks to their best advantage (see Figure 1.5).

In outline, the self-reporting questionnaire output looks as follows:

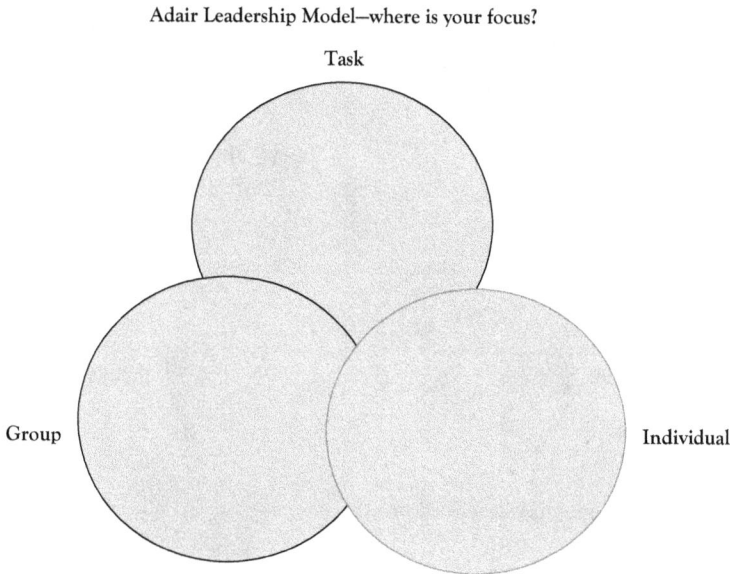

Adair Leadership Model—where is your focus?

Task

Group

Individual

Figure 1.5 Adair leadership model

Your profile is compared to an *ideal* profile very well balanced: you can then see any areas for improvement.

The Questionnaire

The questionnaire used is the Dr. John Adair personal leadership profile available from www.johnadair.co.uk/profiles.html.

You can see the imbalance here—the focus is nearly all tasks. Indeed, in today's fast-moving and in a people-inclusive environment, this is not satisfactory.

All Task, doomed to failure as not involving people—very little will be achieved (see Figure 1.6).

Adair Leadership Model—where is your focus? High task profile showing development requirements for people involvement

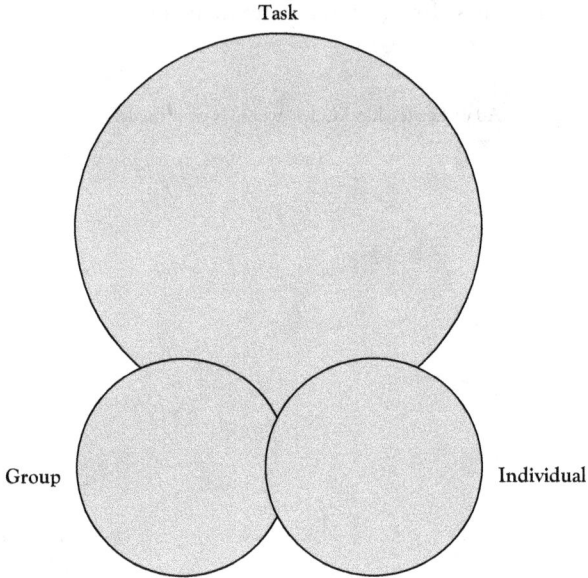

Figure 1.6 *High-task-oriented profile*

Adair Leadership Model—where is your focus?
Very people oriented—but very low task

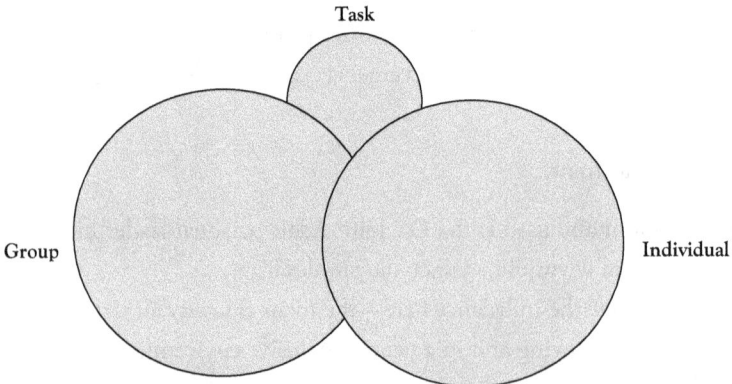

Figure 1.7 *High people focus*

Figure 1.7 shows a very high people focus. A very popular leader who is unlikely to get things done! Getting the balance provides a rounded leader—an inspirational leader who gets things done, involving everyone in the process. It's hard to achieve, but who said being a leader in today's rapidly changing environment would be easy?

Conclusion

The day of the manager is ending. The amazingly fast-changing and newly evolving business world demands people who produce results. Inspirational leaders are needed, those with a future focus and the ability to get the very best from the team(s) they lead. Indeed, an exciting and challenging time ahead. The new leaders required now and for the future are not just at the top of the organization but are at every level (see Figure 1.8). They are defined in five categories:

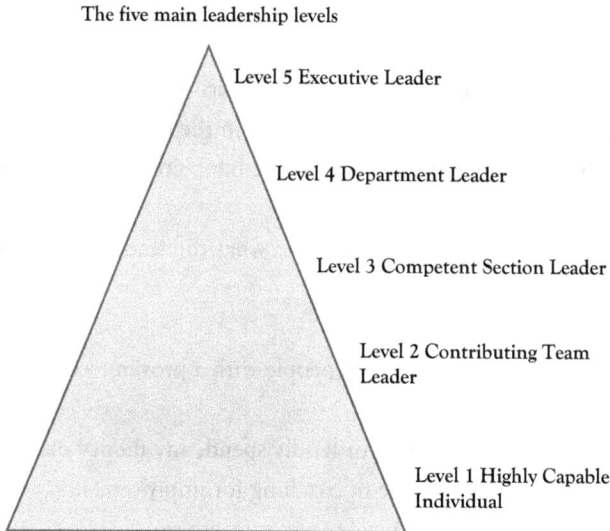

The five main leadership levels

Level 5 Executive Leader

Level 4 Department Leader

Level 3 Competent Section Leader

Level 2 Contributing Team Leader

Level 1 Highly Capable Individual

Figure 1.8 The five levels of leaders

Every successful business will need talented people—already worldwide, they are in short supply. Talented people respect good leaders but do not respond well to strict, old-school managers. The way that talented people are rewarded, motivated, and retained is covered later in this book.

The war on talent is won by investing in people's careers (LHH 12/2022 *Sunday Times*).

In the words of Elon Musk:

It is a mistake to hire huge numbers of people to get a complicated job done. Numbers will never compensate for talent in getting the right answer (two people who don't know something are no better than one), will tend to slow down progress, and will make the task incredibly expensive. (2022)

The leader—the organizational conductor—an interesting example, perhaps.

Any orchestra is comprised of leaders. Each section of the orchestra has a leader; let us call it the department head. They are responsible for hiring the right musicians with the right skill level. They do not employ second-grade people or people who cannot do the job. Of paramount importance is that they can work together seamlessly, and that every performance is perfect.

The leader of the orchestra (the conductor) is just like a CEO in any business. Their job is to bring out the best in the orchestra. The conductor is in the unique position of seeing the big picture, and on every day, creating a masterpiece of music.

This is the leader's role. Just look at what the leader of the orchestra achieves:

- They only employ talented people with a proven record (no second division).
- Orchestras don't spend, or hardly spend, any money on training but allow time in coaching for improvement.
- A high level of trust, loyalty, and purpose exist.
- Good time keeping is evident.
- Normally low turnover.
- High level of participation—you do not see them doing online shopping while working.
- Within the orchestra, there are many leaders—just as in an organization.

- The orchestra performs well even if the conductor is absent. Everyone knows what needs to be done. This is in stark contrast to the manager, who often believes that when they are not there, the wheels will fall off the wagon (Nierenberg, R. 2017).

CHAPTER 2

Managing Performance Productivity

A Review of the Formula Needed for Prime Calculations

You can't manage and get the best from people if you are not a master of performance's primary figures and what constitutes a sustainable competitive improvement. That is what we know as productivity. This is made complex as many issues such as bonus, pay, budgets, competency matrixes, and performance appraisal are governed by other departments. It is very worrying that in a survey in March 2023, reported in the *Times* newspaper, 82 percent of HR managers reported that they did not have effective performance metrices.

Yet, the job of getting things done through others and achieving and exceeding objectives is the leader's job—leadership skill 3.

Leadership skill 3. The leader must have a process to set, measure, and reward objectives to get the best consistent results.

The current increasing pace of change and the need for an agile organization require management to develop projections, for what's needed in the future. What's required explicitly are accurate workforce numbers and organizational shape to deliver impressive results. This applies to both the public and private sectors.

Prime Working Days Formula 10 (PWD)

In nearly all calculations about work, you will need this calculation sooner or later. How many days do people work in your organization?

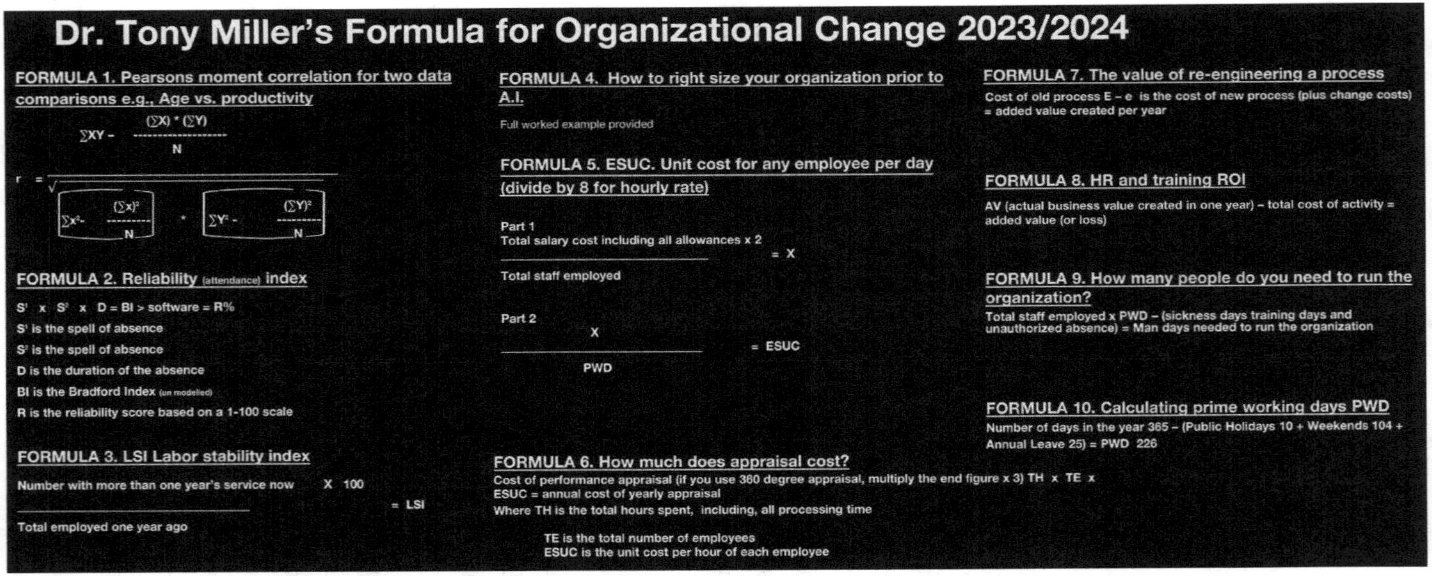

Dr. Tony Miller's Formula for Organizational Change 2023/2024

FORMULA 1. Pearsons moment correlation for two data comparisons e.g., Age vs. productivity

$$r = \frac{\sum XY - \frac{(\sum X) \cdot (\sum Y)}{N}}{\sqrt{\left[\sum X^2 - \frac{(\sum X)^2}{N}\right] \cdot \left[\sum Y^2 - \frac{(\sum Y)^2}{N}\right]}}$$

FORMULA 2. Reliability (attendance) index

$S^1 \times S^1 \times D = BI > software = R\%$

S is the spell of absence

S^1 is the spell of absence

D is the duration of the absence

BI is the Bradford index (un modified)

R is the reliability score based on a 1-100 scale

FORMULA 3. LSI Labor stability index

$$\frac{\text{Number with more than one year's service now}}{\text{Total employed one year ago}} \times 100 = LSI$$

FORMULA 4. How to right size your organization prior to A.I.

Full worked example provided

FORMULA 5. ESUC. Unit cost for any employee per day (divide by 8 for hourly rate)

Part 1
Total salary cost including all allowances x 2 = X

Part 2 $\dfrac{X}{PWD}$ = ESUC

FORMULA 6. How much does appraisal cost?

Cost of performance appraisal (if you use 360 degree appraisal, multiply the end figure x 3) TH x TE x ESUC = annual cost of yearly appraisal

Where TH is the total hours spent, including, all processing time

TE is the total number of employees
ESUC is the unit cost per hour of each employee

FORMULA 7. The value of re-engineering a process

Cost of old process E – e is the cost of new process (plus change costs) = added value created per year

FORMULA 8. HR and training ROI

AV (actual business value created in one year) – total cost of activity = added value (or loss)

FORMULA 9. How many people do you need to run the organization?

Total staff employed x PWD – (sickness days training days and unauthorized absence) = Main days needed to run the organization

FORMULA 10. Calculating prime working days PWD

Number of days in the year 365 – (Public Holidays 10 + Weekends 104 + Annual Leave 25) = PWD 226

Figure 2.1 Essential formula

Standard reply 52 weeks × 5 days = 260 days, but it is not valid or accurate.

How many days do your employees work? The calculation will vary from company to company; an acknowledged average is 226 days a year. When you use the following formula, you will need to adjust the figures for an exact fit for your company.

Days in the year 365 – (Holidays 25 + Public Holidays 10 + Weekends 104) = 226 PWD

The figure of 226 becomes the number of days for productivity calculations, business expansion, or contraction calculations and the basis for calculating the employee standard unit cost (ESUC).

You will use this for rightsizing mainly before implementing AI and for calculations necessary to show the value of remote workers.

What Is the ESUC for Days Worked? Formula 5

The ESUC is the basis of all calculations for efficiency, production costs, and savings. This is one very emotive figure; once you understand how it is calculated, run it past the finance director to get it approved—remember, this is a rough unit cost; it is an average—not an exact figure. It is good enough for us to do a range of calculations and predictions.

A Worked Example of Formula 5

The company employs 3,000 people with a total salary bill that includes pay, overtime, car allowance, housing allowance, and *all* allowances, including medical and any tax contributions. In this example, it amounts to U.S.$125,280,000.00.

You will see in the calculation that the total salary costs are multiplied by two. With the advent of remote working, some, times referred to as homeworking, this may drop to 1.5 or lower.

The factor of two is the actual expenses we can attribute to every employee; training, electricity, facilities, IT, floor space, company vehicles, and so on. *It's an average.*

If you have lots of spare time, you can work this out by looking at the annual accounts, but we use two as the factor for simplicity. There are a few companies where the factor would be higher, such as in Google, Apple, and Facebook.

Remember, you are not the company's mathematics department— you just need working standard figures.

We then divide the top-line total by the number of employees, which gives us X.

X is then divided by 226 (PWD) to give you the ESUC per day, which is the actual cost per day.

$$\frac{X\ (\$83{,}520)}{226\ (\text{PWD})} = \text{ESUC } \$369$$

Divide ESUC by eight to get an hourly rate of U.S.$46.

Understanding these two formulas, 5 and 10, enables you to take a hard look at what people do when they are available for work. The actual cost of U.S.$46.00; it is not what they are paid; it's the actual cost of employment.

I have heard a few comments on calculating the PWD, but the ESUC always looks controversial. Often the word from CFOs is that "it is not the way we do it"—my reply is always the same to this statement: "Well, please show me the formula you use"; of course, there is not one. In any organization with the massive changes that are taking place, cost–benefit and competitor advantage must be top of the agenda.

These specific two calculations are used for:

- Working out and demonstrating the cost to the organization of poor performers
- When doing a tabletop exercise for rightsizing
- When working out the cost-benefit of organizational change and implementation of AI
- The basics for reminding team members of the cost of lost time, specifically lateness and wasted meetings

What Is the Organizational Cost of Poor Performance?

If you ask this simple question, the answer is rarely forthcoming. However, it's not difficult to work out seeing Formulas 5 and 10 and with some basic organizational information.

Two critical questions need to be asked:

- How many people do we have in the three employment categories? Talented, average, and poor performers?
- Then, how many hours do these groups really work?

In a recent study, the answers were very interesting.

As we know, employees are in three categories—poor performers, average performers, and talented.

In our sample organization employing 3,000 people, it was found:

17 percent are talented, a total of 510—they work 6.4 hours a day.

61 percent are average performers, a total of 1,830—they work four hours a day.

22 percent are poor performers, a total of 660—they work one hour a day.

N.B. The hours shown are for actual work done in the context of a 40-hour contractual week. Talented people, in particular, usually work many extra hours out of the contractual week.

As in all organizations, there are other lost time variables. In our test company, we find for each employee.

Average time lost through sickness	10 days per year
Average unauthorized absence	5 days per year
Average for training/conferences	12 days per year
TOTAL extra time lost	**27 days per year per person**

Revised PWD 226 – 27 days = **199 days**

Talented employees PWD 199 × hours worked per day 6.4 × number of employees 510 = total hours worked 649,536

Average employees PWD 199 × hours worked per day 4 × number of employees 1,830 = total hours worked 1,456,680

Poor performers PWD 199 × hours worked per day 1 × number of employees 660 = total hours worked 131,340

Total hours worked per year 649,536 + 1,456,680 + 131,340 = **2,237,556 hours**

What Are We Really Interested In?

Poor performers. We are paying poor performers to work eight hours a day; they work only one hour a day. Lost time amounts to seven hours a day.

7 hours × $46 × 199 (days per year) × 660 people = $42,291,480.00. **The cost of lost production in one year.**

When rightsizing the organization, this group has to go. They account for much of the training budget, take up an excessive amount of management time, and have a positive disruptive effect on the organization. It's worth finding out who hired them; usually, it's low-performing managers/supervisors.

The Critical Path for Measuring Competencies and Performance

The productivity dashboard is a significant leap forward and is far more in tune with what is done to produce *accurate* organizational results. The first move in this measurement many years ago was the key performance indicators. They were a good start, but like competencies, the process rapidly got overcomplicated as various consultancy companies sought to sell the system—warts and all. If one is not careful, key performance indicators can work against the total benefit to the organization.

The Three Productivity Indicators Are the Ones That Really Matter (see Figure 2.2)

Competency, performance, and reliability, and know that we can measure all three. One of the great strengths of the performance dashboard is that it is put on display in each department, so you can see immediately how you are performing throughout the year against the target scores or presets.

Preset standards—without clear goals, employees won't know what really matters.

In other words, management should not recruit anyone below this minimum requirement. The company standard is shown at 70 percent (see Figure 2.3). Any employee falling below that competency score should automatically get training. Once an employee reaches 70 percent (depending on the job), then they are said to have attained the required employment standard.

Time and experience will raise that score.

Should you pay employees for being competent? Not really; this is covered in their basic pay and is assumed that employees are competent

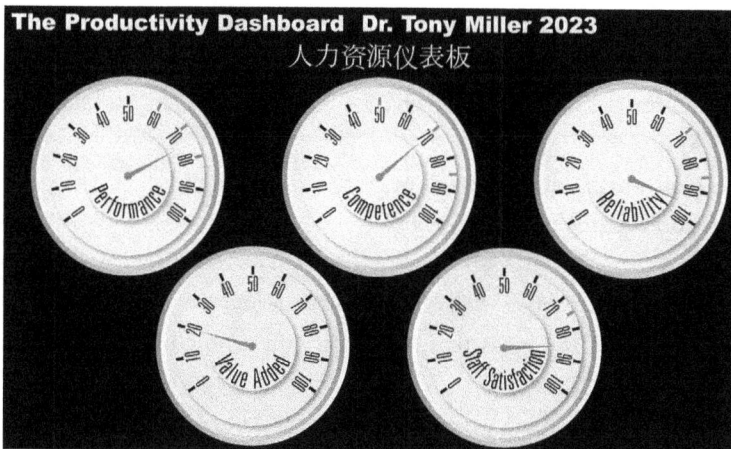

Figure 2.2 Productivity dashboard

Competency

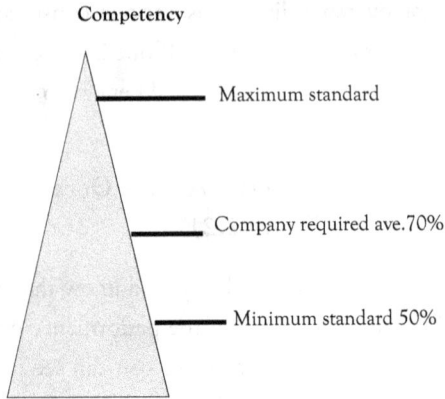

Maximum standard

Company required ave.70%

Minimum standard 50%

Figure 2.3 Competency standards

when you do your professional recruitment. As we improve recruitment, specifically for talented people, it's difficult; you would never recruit anyone who is not fully competent. The exception would be university graduates or college leavers when applying for their first job.

When we look at competencies, we look only at the key, critical competencies. Usually, this would not be more than six. Each competency has about four units, so we are asking managers and line supervisors to measure 24 units per employee. This is reasonable and manageable and can only be done by the immediate line management.

Why is it essential to put competency on our dashboard?

Competencies give the organization three critical features:

1. Competent employees will ensure conformance to standards (quality).
2. Competent employees will be lawful in their work.
3. Competent employees are safe.

Using the dashboard will also give you an inventory of your competency strengths and areas that need attention through the information you gather.

As with performance, competencies need to have presets.

The preset is 50 percent minimum, with the average being 70 percent. These data will allow you to target training with great accuracy as clearly;

anyone scoring under 70 percent would need assistance on the unit concerned.

The presets may vary slightly from company to company, but this is a good starting point, and it is realistic in its assumptions. Time and experience also have a significant impact on your competency scores. This will happen once the employees get to the 70 percent mark, so in practice, there is not really any need to train people whose scores are 70 plus. Time and experience on the job will keep the scores moving upward.

The measurement of key competencies is the leaders' responsibility. The measurement before the appraisal can be carried out in a number of ways:

- By observation
- By simulation
- By third-party observation
- By test
- By the gathering of evidence, written, oral, or film.

Regardless of how it's gathered, the point of recording is recorded on the performance appraisal document (paper or electronic).

A word of advice—keep this data collection system simple and quick.

As 70 to 90 percent of all training will come from these data, training needs can now be automated into an AI system. The software exists to do this, and both competence and performance can be accurately recorded and translated into precise training needs. This will save time and, of course, cost.

Key points about competencies:

- Competence guarantees quality, safety, and conformance to standards. A lack of competency standards in organizations undoubtedly contributed to many financial failures.
- Measure what matters—the units from critical competencies only.
- Set up standards—minimum, company standard, and top-end competency scores.

This will clarify your organization's competency levels, strengths, and weaknesses. To make this a success, you need to involve all of the senior staff to get not only the buy-in from them but also a good understanding of how the competency system works. Don't pay a bonus on competency levels—that's what you pay for with your basic salary payment. Competency will increase with time on the job—this is often overlooked.

How to Measure and Automate Performance Data

Performance is raw output, how much we do. Performance is measured in many ways, including the following:

- Speed
- Time
- Efficiency
- Unit cost
- Volume

Most companies are overstaffed by 15 to 20 percent. This has been specifically evident during the COVID-19 crisis. And, of course, by a much higher percentage in the public sector. Published figures by the UK government showed that there were 50 percent too many people in the public sector. It was reported by McKenzie Consulting that one in 10 employees in the health service could be dispensed with. In a survey of public sector employees, 89 percent felt that budgets and public spending were managed inefficiently.

What kind of expected performance should be made very clear in the contract of employment, although companies should seek legal counsel in this regard as employment law statutes vary geographically on this issue. On the other hand, performance levels above those required should be locked into a bonus or reward system. If the original criteria are correctly set, it should be difficult for employees to do more simultaneously because, in theory, they are working at their optimal level (see Figure 2.4). So, you will need to decide—bonus or overtime—but not both.

Performance–preset standards

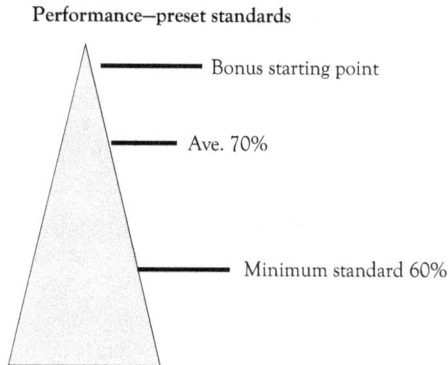

Figure 2.4 Performance standards

Performance expectations (above the required performance) should be established during the performance appraisal and updated throughout the year.

Measuring performance can be done in three different ways; these are approached depending on the type of business you work in, the country you are employed in, and finally, the culture of the company or organization that you are part of.

How to set objectives to get massive results is described in Chapter 4.

The first method can be done in three ways:

1. Performance measured by time worked. This works well if you have managers who do manage. Also, certain cultures are very work-focused, and when they are at work—they work hard. This mainly applies to China, where it's hard work and by the hour.
2. Performance through individual target setting. This is a real winner, but it carries with it a big warning. Correctly set and monitored targets with big bonuses produce massive results, provided:
   a. At the end of the year, the bonuses are not subjected to a forced ranking, which is an enormous demotivator, with staff knowing that they have been cheated.
   b. The bonus must be subjected to the average competence and reliability scores being achieved.
   The bonus scheme and methodology of how it works are explained in detail in Chapter 6.

    c. That the bonus is directly aligned with organizational achievement. Not based on your position or job title.

3. Performance through team target setting. This has the same criteria as the aforementioned very much but uses a hopper bonus scheme where all participants (the team) need to meet the score requirement for competence and reliability before any member of the team can earn any bonus.

Self-motivated staff—these employees are painstakingly recruited and know what needs to be done. They require little motivation or supervision and work whatever hours are needed. They are typically rewarded via some form of share/stock option scheme. The label we give this group is talented people.

Another method is the managed workforce employed but not trusted. Management runs a strict and inflexible routine. In this instance, performance is achieved by hours worked, the manager taking responsibility for prescribing work and ensuring it is done within the time allocated.

The most abused is the setting of objectives and stretch targets. The old-style managers are not good at doing this and are constantly undermined by having forced ranked bonus schemes determining who gets what bonus at the end of the year. A consistent theme in performance—it must be measured.

Regardless of which of the three schemes you use, the approach for measurement is the same as for competency. Management needs to set minimum company standards and top-end figures for performance.

As with competency (quality), no bonus or additional payments should be made for anything below the required average standard. If required performance is not achieved, then employees' basic salaries should be reduced. Check this out carefully as it may not be legally possible, although I think it is morally right. All of this highlights the need for adopting thorough recruitment practices; for getting guidance on this, look at how good Google is at this—and look at their bottom-line performance figures.

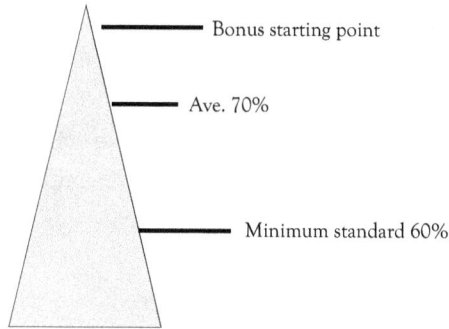

Figure 2.5 Setting performance standards

You may be wondering why productivity is not 100 percent on our chart. Well, two very separate components affect this. The first is time. In a 40-hour week—no one can work 40 hours. We have PT&C (Pee, Tea and Cigarette) time plus a lunch break. So at best, the working week will be only 32 hours of available time.

Poor overall performance is compensated for by the old-style managers who demand more staff, resulting in overstaffed organizations. Very evident during COVID-19, and in 2023, the massive reductions in staffing levels.

Gathering performance data is, of course, done at performance appraisal. We use the same process that we do for competency information.

Now what's important is that both competency and performance are on linear scales of 1 to 100, perfect for AI to pick up at a later date.

Reliability—What Is It? How to Measure and Improve It?

Reliability is a dimension of value that is very rarely measured by workforce management. So, what is reliability, and why should we take it seriously? We already know the costs of an employee and what that cost is per day. We also see the cost of an employee per hour. Reliability is a measurement of whether or not that person attends for the hours that they are paid.

Unreliable people tend to commence work late, often leave early, and have a remarkably high level of unsubstantiated sick leave.

The two critical areas for us to focus on are our sickness and unsubstantiated days off. This is either from uncertified illness or other reasons. The terminology makes this authorized or unauthorized absenteeism, but the global title used is reliability. Why we need to get on top of this issue is that it costs lots of money directly and hurts employee morale indirectly. That is why, measuring reliability is increasingly an essential factor in workforce management and reporting the cost of unreliable people is a significant business cost factor.

When a public organization in the UK was investigated, it was found that employees were shown to have had 895,000 days off (was this sick leave?). With 50,000 employees, that equates to each employee having 17.9 days off on average every year.

Fortunately, mathematically, it is possible to calculate by individual, section, or department the direct cost of reliability. This can also be projected using our predictive workforce management tools showing the cost over 5, 10, and 15 years. For all organizations, this figure is so significant that it cannot be ignored.

For example, if one person comes to work late every day (just 30 minutes) and has 14 uncertified sick days in a year, then what is the cost in reliability for this employee for one year?

Lateness $46 × 0.5 × 226 = $5,198
Uncertified sickness $46 × 8 × 14 = $5,152
Total cost = $10,350 per employee

If 20 percent of our 3,000-strong workforce falls into this category, then the real cost per year is:

600 × $10,350 = **$6,210,000**

So, for our three time scales of 5, 10, and 15 years, that is:

5 × $6,210,000 = $31,050,000
10 × $6,210,000 = $62,100,000
15 × $6,210,000 = $93,150,000

These are very conservative figures from work on reliability carried out over many years. If this does not grab your attention, do the calculation based on A City Council's figures: 17.9 days off each year for each of the 50,000 people? An AI system would never have allowed this to occur; there is a lot to be said for automated processes.

Measurement of reliability – new tools = great results

When gathering data, we use Formula 2 and then the figures are converted into a linear scale so that we can correlate them for other comparative work.

Using your facts, you can now do a benchmark to find out how reliable your employees are and what's the cost to the organization. It's management's job to rectify the fault if you have a big issue here—not yours. You have identified the problem, costed it out, and provided the management information on the cost to the organization. Ongoing monitoring will make this a critical human capital measurement factor.

It would be prudent to come up with a figure of where you expect the organization to be on the chart—100 percent is unrealistic.

Thus, using an existing formula (the Bradford formula), we have mathematically adjusted the output so that the final scores run on a 0 to 100 scale (see Figure 2.6), with the indicators showing when counseling is needed when a first verbal warning is given. Then, the next written warning is given, and when a final written warning is given, dismissal is given. AI will, of course, do this automatically.

Reliability, with competence measurement and productivity measurement, can now be measured as one integrated system; AI will integrate and report on the results. The data are fed into this program, and the appropriate actions to be taken are displayed to the management so that there can be no oversight, slippage, or *forgetfulness* to take action.

As mentioned before, reliability is one of three key indicators that together equal productivity. It is essential that any decisions on increments, bonuses, allowances, or promotions be taken only after viewing the total picture. Very often, reliability is not taken into account during interviews or for selection and promotion. Poor reliability has a marked

Measuring reliability

100	=	0
75	=	96.5
50	=	193
25	=	289.5
0	=	386

Figure 2.6 0–100 scale set against Bradford formula

effect on other employees' motivation to such an extent that it severely impacts organizational efficiency if it is left unchecked.

The value of time and people—essential calculations and information

The cost of poor reliability is enormous not only in straight financial terms, for example, in the matter of paying an employee's salary, but also regarding missed deadlines, slippages, and low-quality work. Therefore, I am sure you can see that reliability is a crucial indicator and essential for our dashboard.

Can poor reliability be identified? Significant evidence exists that likely poor reliability can be identified using personality profilers. On OCEAN, low Cs and high Ns need watching.

Other research has been carried out regarding the impact of job satisfaction and absenteeism on an employee, and there seems to be clear evidence of positive correlations between high-frequency absenteeism (many short absences from work) and dissatisfaction in the job. This shows the importance of doing regular staff satisfaction surveys to ensure and measure the relationship between absenteeism and the staff satisfaction scale. This is so important that it features on our dashboard productivity indicator scale.

Linking Measurement to Performance Schemes

> *The leader must have a process to set, measure, and reward objectives to get the best consistent results.*

This is Leadership skill 3, as discussed in Chapter 1.

This isn't easy to do as some of the processes (pay and bonuses) are controlled by others. Also, performance appraisal, which is supposed to be the biggest goal-setting process. Rarely is any effort made to measure its cost-effectiveness or efficiency.

Competence scores, performance scores, and reliability are all factors to use as a precursor to entering the bonus scheme. They make the rules very clear and transparent to all—to ensure the requirements are visible. It would be impossible for a poor performer to get into the bonus ladder. Likewise, only about 40 percent of average performers would qualify. The bonus pot is therefore very big and will go to those who actually put in the work and produce results (see Figure 2.7).

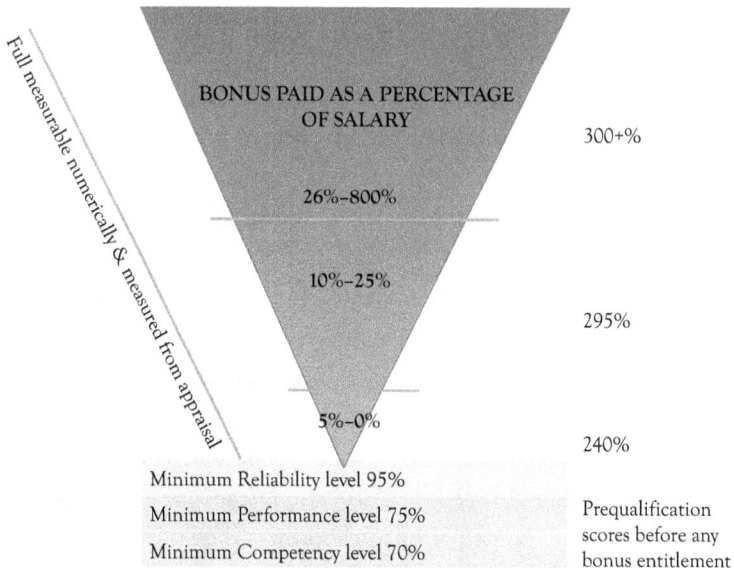

BONUS PAID AS A PERCENTAGE OF SALARY

300+%

26%–800%

10%–25%

295%

5%–0%

240%

Full measurable numerically & measured from appraisal

Minimum Reliability level 95%

Minimum Performance level 75%

Minimum Competency level 70%

Prequalification scores before any bonus entitlement

Figure 2.7 Hopper bonus chart

Pay Big Bonuses

From a motivational impact, it's better to pay bonuses quarterly or half-yearly if this can be managed. Don't keep bonus payments secret; the best should be well paid, and the organization should be proud of them, encouraging others to excel as well.

There is a fundamental paradigm change—organizations will be shifting from paying for knowledge to paying for what you do, producing results.

Some Conclusions and Things to Reflect On

1. Poor performers are too expensive to tolerate. Poor performers: they need to leave the organization. Perhaps along with the people who recruited them.

2. Make recruiters responsible for their recruitment decisions. Outsourcing recruitment is often a bad decision. Get the hiring manager a tattoo "Never let another Bozo into the company."

3. Managing and getting the best from your employees requires transparent and clearly understood policies and systems. Talented people need guidelines to work best and are an exceptional group. As a group, they respond well to a participative leadership style of management. "Help People Reach Their Full Potential Catch Them Doing Something Right."—Kenneth H. Blanchard.

4. Focus on what's essential, competence, *performance*, and reliability.

5. Pay *big* bonuses to those who are talented and who *do* the work (Chapter 5).

6. Master data so you can lead with confidence and add value to your organization.

7. You need to master and be in control of your budget. This may seem obvious, but getting to grips and thoroughly understanding and managing your budget is a critical skill. As each organization seems to do this differently, here is some general advice that may be of use.

   a. Make sure you know exactly how your budget has been constructed. If you have inherited it from someone else, be particularly careful. Some points to check, was the budget built from a zero base, or is it following a standard format? Make sure you know and understand each budget heading. If it's a revenue budget, how often are the spend figures available, weekly or monthly? What is in your capital budget, how does it work, and what is the exact figure going to be at the end of the financial year? Over how many years is your capitalized cost to be spread? These are your depreciation costs, and they are typically spread over many years.

b. Consider keeping a spreadsheet in your department that totals weekly expenditure for the year to date. Then you have an exact figure of your costs as they occur.

c. How will payroll (your employee costs) appear, monthly or at the end of the year? likewise bonus payments. If you're using goodies (Chapter 6), how will they be funded—as part of payroll or out of your budget?

d. Help finance departments. When your budget is approved, explain how it will be spent. For sure, it won't be spent evenly in 12 nice convenient segments.

e. Consider making your team responsible for segments of the budget, the more involved they are, the more careful they will be for what they spend. Trust them, but make them accountable. A useful maxim here is to remember *"Treat people like children— they behave like children. Treat people like adults; they behave like adults."*

CHAPTER 3

The Rebirth of Artificial Intelligence

The Immense and Unstoppable Progress of AI

It's hard to imagine a business or area of work that will not be touched by AI in the next few years. AI has expanded and improved so quickly that its advancement and achievements are almost incomprehensible. Yet many still see AI as one of those high-tech things that won't catch on. Progress is moving so fast that organizations cannot afford to wait; changes will not wait—for sure.

Apple's Tim Cook: AI will "Affect Every Product and Service We Have" (2023).

AI has come to the fore because of three significant factors.

1. The first is what we refer to as *big data*. We now can manipulate vast quantities of stored data and, with these data, can produce predictive outcomes. What's been in the press often is how our digital footprint is now being used. From the moment you ever switched on a computer, mobile phone, or tablet, or used a credit card, data have been recorded, stored, shuffled, packaged, and sold by companies such as Axiom. Big data are now available to all.
2. The next is affordable *high-powered computing*. Processing speeds and storage have increased, and computing prices have dramatically dropped. We now have quantum computers, some of which allow free access.
3. The final is the emergence of *deep learning systems*. These systems start learning by themselves using cognitive learning without the need for old-style programming.

The formula then is:

BD + HPC + DLS = AI

You will hear the term *neuro networks* being used quite frequently these days, so here is an attempt to explain what they are. We have the straightforward mathematical computation of an input, weighting, and addition, which gives us a mathematical output.

AI, particularly deep learning, develops things further and has made rapid strides in a relatively short span of time.

In AI, we connect many layers of neurons; today, we have millions of these as paired inputs and, likewise, a multitude of outputs. Deep neural networks are vast and very complicated; the big breakthrough that happened recently is that these networks now have the cognitive ability to process; this has caused a dramatic improvement and change. It can be called *self-thinking*. The program automatically alters the weighting and keeps self-adjusting until it achieves predetermined outcomes. The person credited for this is probably Geoffrey Hinton, the company that has been most instrumental in exploiting this is Google.

We use algorithms to instruct AI and get it to solve problems. An algorithm is a detailed series of instructions for carrying out an operation or solving a problem. In a nontechnical context, we use algorithms.

Some recent facts to think about:

- AI will be one of the significant factors in reducing job numbers globally. It's already happened. Look at the numbers, ironically the first big job losses were in the IT industry. Figures available show that job losses in IT are running at 1,400 a week in the United States. No area seems safe, banking, financial services, the car industry, Amazon and Disney all shedding masses of employees.

The highest *At Risk* groups being:

1. *Tech jobs (coders, computer programmers, software engineers, data analysts)*
2. *Media jobs (advertising, content creation, technical writing, journalism)*
3. *Legal industry jobs (paralegals, legal assistants)*

4. *Market research analysts*
5. *Teachers*
6. *Finance jobs (financial analysts, personal financial advisors)*
7. *Traders*
8. *Graphic designers*
9. *Accountants*
10. *Customer service agents*

Source: Mok and Zinkula (2023).

- We will unlikely see employment levels recover, specifically for average and poor performers, due to the declining cost of robotics and AI innovations in how we do things.
- COVID-19 was a wakeup call and showed the world a different and cheaper way to do work.
- AI is now fashioning the way we work—it is different.
- AI will manage the way we are individually monitored at work and probably socially.
- Intelligent robots could replace 30 percent of the work force by 2030.
- 77 percent of us regularly interact with AI—but only 33 percent think they do.
- ChatGPT 4 from Sam Altman (2023) will change the way we get information and solve problems and aid in being more innovative. As this is going to be one of the biggest changes to how we get information, here is a brief description of what it is:

The Product: ChatGPT 4

- It's made by a company called OpenAI, which has been at the forefront of making generative AI available to the masses (Sam Altman).
- **What it does:** A writing tool that responds to queries and requests with text that looks like it was made by a human.
- **How you get it:** It's free to use. https://chat.openai.com/auth/login, but it has been so popular that sometimes it's unavailable during peak hours.

Open AI plans to charge people a fee per month for a commercial version that's faster and always available.

- People are finding all sorts of real-world uses for ChatGPT, from drafting screenplays to writing computer code. ChatGPT had *more than 100 million users within the first two months of its launch.*
- ChatGPT can be easy to talk to, but it's currently rectifying issues it has with math, often strangely confident about being wrong.
- Using ChatGPT for anything other than personal experimentation comes with lots of ethical concerns.
- You will find ChatGPT will become an essential tool at work.
- Some departments will find most of their work superseded by the immediacy and accuracy of ChatGPT 4.

Other major innovations of change are DALL-E specializing in image creation and adaption. New on the street in 2023 is API; this Adept AI specifically is a tool to aid knowledge workers to boost their use and deeper understanding of everyday software tools (see Figure 3.1).

Facial recognition for security and employee tracking is already in place, with an accuracy of 99.2 percent. On February 2, 2020, LG employees were able to pass through company gates without stopping. The company announced that LG CNS had deployed a facial recognition gate control service that runs on AI software at its headquarters in Seoul.

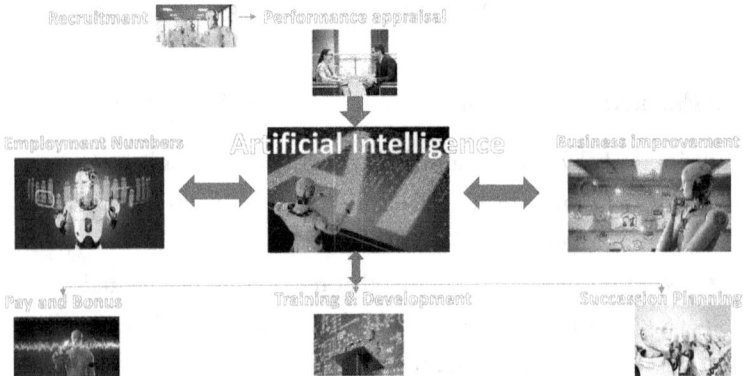

Figure 3.1 The way AI will manage work

This was achieved in collaboration with the Chinese AI firm Sense-Time, which uses a designated reader to identify a face, authenticate an employee, and open the gate within 0.3 seconds, according to LG CNS. The company added that the facial recognition gate has an accuracy of over 99 percent and can identify faces 2 meters from its reader even if the person wears a mask, glasses, makeup, or positions their head at an angle.

- Seven out of 10 governments currently use facial recognition; AI-based.
- On facial recognition, it advances by the day; in 2021, Asst. Professor Kosinski published a paper detailing the fantastic advances in facial recognition.

Ubiquitous facial recognition technology can expose individuals' political orientation, as faces of liberals and conservatives consistently differ. A facial recognition algorithm was applied to naturalistic images of 1,085,795 individuals to predict their political orientation by comparing their similarity to faces of liberal and conservative others. Political orientation was correctly classified in 72% of liberal–conservative face pairs, remarkably better than chance (50%), human accuracy (55%), or one afforded by a 100-item personality questionnaire (66%). Accuracy was similar across countries (the US, Canada, and the U.K.), environments (Facebook and dating websites), and when comparing faces across samples. Accuracy remained high (69%) even when controlling for age, gender, and ethnicity. Given the widespread use of facial recognition, our findings have critical implications for the protection of privacy and civil liberties.

Robots will be able to do everything better than us…I am not sure exactly what to do about this. This is really the scariest problem to me.

—Elon Musk

Source: Apple AI news 12.2.2020.

A fast-growing and exciting area, neuro technologies are based on the principles of the human nervous system and modeled on the human brain. NeuroTech can help researchers understand brain function and dysfunction and can help doctors treat neurological disorders. Some NeuroTech applications focus on enhancing cognitive performance, improving sleep, and improving brain health for longevity. Advances in AI could revolutionize NeuroTech over the next decade.

> Over U.S.$19 billion has been invested in NeuroTech companies in the last 20 years.
>
> There are currently over 200 NeuroTech companies in the world reported in *Apple News*.
>
> The country with the most NeuroTech companies is the United States with 121. Canada has 14, the UK has 13, Switzerland has eight, Israel has seven, and France has six.
>
> There are currently over 200 NeuroTech investors in the world.
>
> The country with the most NeuroTech investors is the United States with 136. Japan and the UK both have 10, Canada has seven, and China and France both have six.
>
> The value of NeuroTech patents was U.S.$2 billion in 2015.

Massive Advances in Computing—of Interest Only to the Techies

Frontier, a supercomputer built using Hewlett–Packard Enterprise (HPE) architecture and equipped with advanced micro devices (AMD) processors, outperformed Fugaku to become the world's fastest supercomputer according to the Top 500 list of world's most powerful supercomputers. For the techies, the supercomputer, built for the U.S. Department of Energy's Oak Ridge National Laboratory (ORNL), has reached the Linmark benchmark score of 1.1 exaflops, making it the world's first supercomputer to break the exascale speed barrier. Fugaku, installed at the RIKEN Center for Computational Science in Kobe, Japan, has a Linmark benchmark score of 442 petaflops (1 exaflop is equivalent to 1,000 petaflops).

> *Frontier is a first-of-its-kind system that was envisioned by technologists, scientists and researchers to unleash a new level of capability*

to deliver open science, A.I. (artificial intelligence) and other break-throughs, that will benefit humanity.

—Justin Hotard, EVP and G.M., HPC & AI,
at HPE, said in a statement. May 31, 2022

Much about AI was explained in the book *A.I. and Remote Working published by Business Expert Press 2021/22 ISBN: 9781637421215 by Dr. Tony Miller.*

We are all aware that we have biases. This shows up at interviews and performance appraisals and can become a big issue when allocating bonuses. This human trait of bias has appeared in AI systems and has been a problem. Recent research has indicated that this can almost be eliminated using synthetic data. The data themselves are artificially created by the computer rather than collected from real-world data sources. It almost seems like the work of science fiction; it's happening right now, *as reported by Sam Forsdick.*

Using OCEAN and the preferred profiling system, IBM Watson Personality Insights provides a service where they can supply an employer with an OCEAN profile; all they need is a sample of handwriting or a sound bite of the person's voice. Their AI program will do the rest. This service used to be available to everyone—now I understand it's really for corporate use only.

The Changing World of Work and the Essential Techniques to Keep the Organization in Shape

A quick historical view of organizations and progress.

It was Adam Smith who first set out the ideas of how people should be managed. Please remember that back in that time, in 1760, the majority of the agricultural workforce was illiterate. Many have spent their lives in agricultural work, and the start of the Industrial Revolution changed to a new type of occupation and a very different way of working. Although it's hard to imagine it now, it must have been very stressful at that time. Days of toiling in the fields doing simple repetitive work was rapidly replaced by factory work, governed by strict timekeeping and output.

Smith's ideas were first adopted by a company called Arkwright based in Cromford in the UK. The workforce had to be managed, and two new jobs were created. The first was that of a *supervisor*. As the name suggested, it was somebody who had super vision. The supervisor in those days was only marginally brighter than the persons they were supervising, and the job was primarily to watch the workers and ensure they didn't wander off and were kept fully engaged at their place of work. The ratio at that time was the famous 1:7. As the supervisors were neither that reliable nor that clever, they needed to be watched as well, and so a new job was invented—that of a *manager*. The manager's job was to watch the supervisors and make sure they did what they were supposed to do. As there were so many managers, it was necessary then to have a senior manager to manage the managers, and so forth. This was how the organization was created and management ratios established.

It is amazing how little progress was made between 1771 and 1980. During this period, there was only a slight improvement in supervisory ratios, from 1:7 to 1:8. The significant changes happened in the 1990s. With the worldwide introduction of the Internet, better schooling, and university education, we suddenly had a far more intelligent workforce. Supervisory ratios throughout the organization started to change, and we started to see companies operating at 1:15 and 1:20. In the late 1990s, some companies were operating with ratios of 1:50. All of this is made possible by continually improving intelligence and a better-informed workforce.

Gone were the days of only getting information from your line manager or supervisor; the Internet has revolutionized the way that we learn and access information as the World Wide Web provided a learning tool for everybody, so the universal use of television widened people's horizons internationally.

The world is now (more or less) stable, and the global economy is fully established. The world has become one enormous supermarket. The breaking down of international barriers to travel has meant we have seen a mass mobilization of workforces on a truly global scale.

With such a well-educated international workforce, we must ask the question, "have we maximized the organization in terms of how people are managed?" For most organizations, the answer must be *no*!

This is an area where new leadership must excel, and if you're looking to get a strategic advantage, then the whole area of how people are led and managed needs to change. There is an interesting correlation between intelligence and supervision. Intelligent people seem to need little, if any, supervision, whereas poorly educated people seemed to be little better than their forebears back in 1771. The only thought you need to give this is whether you are dealing with predominantly stupid people in the organization or whether you have recruited and maximized on getting the best of the best. If the latter is the case, then you have every possibility of making a substantial contribution to improving organizational efficiency, and at the same time, maximizing employee satisfaction with the work that they do.

As I have indicated before, the manager and that type of role have really reached its zenith, and that was in the late 1990s, the role was replaced by that of the inspirational leader. Although these sound like fancy words, they are two different jobs, both of which can be allocated to a specific time in history. Before the 1990s, it was 100 percent of the domain of the manager; since the year 2014, the fundamental requirement in successful organizations is to recruit and retain leaders, as discussed in Chapter 1. Looking at critical processes within any organization, it is vital to regularly examine what we do and why we are doing it. The rate of change is so fast that it is dangerous to slip behind the tidal wave of change.

Some areas to look at include:

- Hiring—a complete upgrade on the process of maximizing personality profiling and testing—any methods to ensure you employ the best. Make recruiters responsible and accountable for their recruitment decisions. Use a process that works. It must include testing and personality profiling, both of which can be accessed remotely. Most of the recruitment will be replaced by ChatGPT, and it is estimated it will do 71 percent of the recruitment process.
- Organizational shape. Is the organization designed for the future, or are its design and Adam Smith–based pyramidal structure dating back to 1760?

Productivity over time

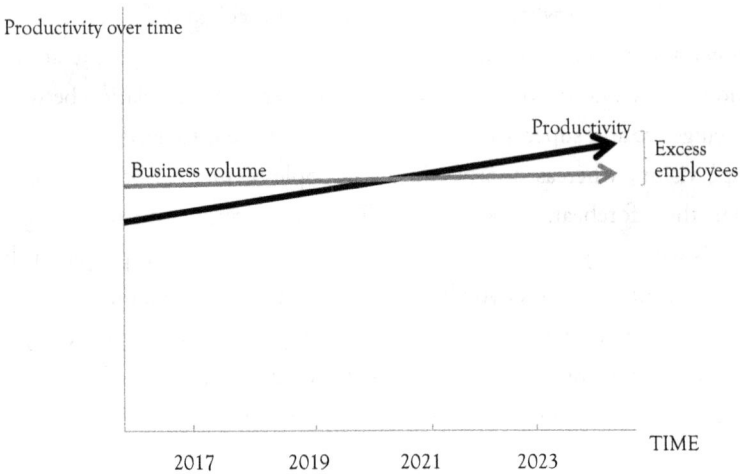

Figure 3.2 Productivity over time

- Do a desktop exercise to see if your organization is correctly staffed. Rightsizing, explained later, is a crucial management tool. Critical if you are to run an effective, efficient organization. Training claims it's a tool to improve productivity. Experience with age claims to be responsible for productivity improvement. Old-style managers claim they drive up productivity. If the organizational workload were stable then year on year, the organization would need fewer people. Curious, don't you think?

Actions Needed

- There has never been a better time to re-engineer existing processes. Renew them or scrap them. What worked in the past will have little value in the future.
- Completely rewrite conditions of contract—also your employee handbook. Most of the latter were written to cover every eventuality associated with poor performers. In the age of talent, we must have appropriate guidelines—that's all.
- When we set targets, they are primarily based on setting SMART objectives Circa 1981; we have moved on since then and need to use a much different approach—Chapter 4.

- An overhaul of performance appraisal's purpose, effectiveness, and cost-effectiveness is long overdue. It's a costly process and rarely is it tested to show if it adds any measurable bottom-line value to the organization.

Organizations are moving away from the Adam Smith style of organization to more people-centric designed organizations. Organizations that have very few managers and very little formal structure. Before you catch yourself saying, "It won't work" or "we are not ready for it yet," here are some interesting facts:

- The first unwitting creator of the people-centric organization was William Shockley. It started in 1956; Shockley spawned a new way of working and a new way of hiring people. Much later, following the Shockley model were Intel, Apple, Facebook, Microsoft, and Google. What they all have in common, they are all immensely successful. Apple was America's first trillion-dollar company.

If you want people to succeed in today's environment, you need to provide a workplace for them to excel. With talented people, this means listening to what they want.

When Apple built its new headquarters, it wanted an environment that would aid its employees to excel. The headquarters was called Apple Park and was one of the world's most expensive buildings costing over U.S.$5 million to construct. The circular construction and design maximized light with a fantastic amount of glass on the external and internal walls. This projected the feeling of tranquility and provided everywhere a beautiful vista wherever you looked—the planting of 9,000 indigenous trees as part of the exceptional landscaping.

Sticking with Apple, the vision was not how cheap can we build this; instead, the cost will be repaid by our highly motivated employees—a different concept, don't you think?

Google, some years before, had produced the Google complex, designed by geeks for geeks. With every convenience on-site—very high productivity levels—why go home? It's all at Google. Interestingly, the most unusual of the Google complexes is sited in Zurich, Switzerland, built to satisfy the requirements of the Google employees. Exciting features include a lounge with a massive aquarium, a fire pole, as it is quicker to get from one floor to another, and a slide that takes you straight into the restaurant!

The purpose of these innovations at work is to retain talented people and, more importantly, provide an environment they want that will be suitable for them to excel. Looking at their financial performance—it works!

The new world of work requires massive change; be a leader, not a follower.

How to Rightsize Any Organization or Department— End-to-End Worked Example

Another "How to do it tool." Regardless of your humanitarian view, AI, remote working, and process redesign will mean you need a lot fewer people. You can agonize over this as much as you like, but it is inevitable and has already happened.

The old way of doing this used to be downsizing. Downsizing was needed by organizations that had lost control of the employees required to run the organization.

Organic growth of any organization is a reality; it makes no difference if that organization is in the public or the private sector, and the endless expansion of the organization's human resources happens. There are five key reasons why:

- The organization's business grows; therefore, it needs more people (this is often a false assumption).
- Managers greed to expand their empires or just that they want personally to do less work.
- Employees who don't do the work they are paid for; hence, more people are needed; this group is what we refer to as poor performers.

- The lack of accurate workforce planning and forecasting resulting in workforce numbers not being in complete synchronization with actual business needs.
- Lack of action in taking responsibility for organizational design.
- A worldwide trend in employee numbers reducing, which commenced in 2023.

Downsizing is a term used in workforce planning to significantly alter the organization's structure. It is usually done to both symmetrical and asymmetrical organizations.

Downsizing is a risky business as it involves taking out whole layers of management. Downsizing usually is, but not always, preceded by doing business process re-engineering.

The key to successful downsizing is to remove layers of management in the organization by finding out the answer to a straightforward question.

Where in the Organization Is the Work Done?

Although the question sounds simple—it is often not that easy to find in the organization. Every layer claims, "This is where the work is done."

Once you have established the truth, you can remove the layers and completely restructure the organization by delayering.

Benefits (UK Example)

- 28 percent improvement in productivity
- Less management

To reduce the risks, time taken, and cost, *rightsizing* is now the preferred option.

The rightsizing exercise is always interesting as it gives you a reality check on the organization's size. This is essential for AI and should be done before any AI or process re-engineering is considered. This gives you an insight as to what's possible right from the start.

Rightsizing is quick; often, from design to implementation, it can be done in four months. The desktop exercise typically takes just a few weeks. Compare this with downsizing, which is done in one to two years.

As all of the current innovations require massive change, rightsizing makes sense if the benefits are to be fully exploited. It is essential for those in leadership roles to clearly understand how rightsizing works, and that it can be done as an in-house exercise without having to use consultants.

To better explain how it works and give a clear understanding, the following end-to-end example, which is based on a real company, helps calculate the right size of any department or organization.

Rightsizing—The Mathematics Involved, and Why It Is Needed Now

A Harris poll carried out in March 2023 showed how many jobs are most likely at risk in 2023 from ChatGPT. The results are so significant that they can't be ignored, neither can the fact that so many organizations, particularly in the public sector, are overstaffed. Some of the results from the survey are as follows:

Data analysis	77 percent
Data entry and processing	75 percent
Media and communications	74 percent
PR	72 percent
Customer service roles	71 percent
Administrative roles	71 percent
Hiring-related tasks	71 percent

Add this to the overstaffing issue the impact of remote working and poor performers in the organization and you can see how essential rightsizing is for the new leadership to tackle.

Step 1

In the organization we are using, for example, we have 3,000 employees. All the work is done each year—so how many hours are worked?

Most CEOs and CFOs will come up with the same answer.

Working hours per week 40 × Weeks in a year 52 × Number of workers 3,000 = 6,240,000

We have an assumption that all the work is being done by our 3,000 employees, and we pay for it, and it takes 6,240,000 hours.

Step 2

To get a more accurate figure, we know that we need to calculate the work done by using the prime working days formula (PWD).

PWD 226 days × Hours worked per day 8 hours × Number of employees 3,000 = **5,424,000 hours** worked. A big difference from our original assumption.

Step 3

As in all organizations, there are other lost time variables. In our test company, we find an average for each employee.

Average time lost through sickness   10 days per year
Average unauthorized absence   5 days per year
Average for training/conferences   12 days per year
TOTAL extra time lost   **27 days per year per person**
Revised PWD 226 – 27 days = 199 days
Actual hours worked in our company.
Days 199 × Hours per day 8 × employees 3,000 = **4,776,000 hours**

Step 4

As we know, employees are in three categories—poor performers, average performers, and talented.

We also know from a large survey done how much work they do.

In our organization, in a 40-hour contractual week:

17 percent are talented, total 510—they work 6.4 hours a day

61 percent are average performers, total 1,830—they work 4 hours a day

22 percent are poor performers, total 660—they work 1 hour a day

Talented PWD 199 × Hours worked per day 6.4 × Number of employees 510 = total hours worked 649,536

Average workers PWD 199 × Hours worked per day 4 × Number of employees. 1,830 = total hours worked 1,456,680

Poor performers PWD 199 × Hours worked per day 1 × Number of employees 660 = total hours worked 131,340

Total hours worked per year 649,536 + 1,456,680 + 131,340 = **2,237,556 Hours**

Step 5

We now know all the work done in our organization was done by 3,000 employees working **2,237,556 hours**, although we are paying them for **6,240,000 hours**.

The question the management team must address is exactly how many hours a day do you expect your employees to work. In our company, it was decided that all employees should work seven hours a day.

Therefore, if PWD is 226, the final calculation would be:

In this desktop exercise, we have established that our company can be run using a total of 1,414 employees—this is an absolute minimum. In reality, it was agreed just over 2,000 people were needed rather than the 3,000 currently employed.

---

a) 226 Prime working days × 7 hours a day = Hours each employee is expected to do real work each year **1,582**.

b) Now, we are going to divide our hours per year for each employee into our actual total hours worked to give the number of employees needed to run our company.

$$\frac{2{,}237{,}556}{1{,}582} = 1{,}414 \text{ rightsized figure. Actual number currently employed } 3{,}000$$

To answer the seemingly impossible question—how many people do we need to run the organization? The answer can be achieved by using rightsizing techniques. The big benefit here is that it can be done as a table-top modeled exercise, so you have reasonable data to work with. This is also a low risk regarding the final decision on how many people you will incorporate your safety margin. In our example, we went with 2,000. It is showing an overstaffing of 1,000 people.

Should Every Department Be a Profit Center— Even in the Public Sector?

New leaders have a golden opportunity to rethink the way things are done at work and how our people see the value of the work they do on a daily basis. The concept is to make each department a value center. At the end of each reporting period, each department head lists out work or ideas that have been put into operation and the value in financial terms to the organization.

The principle of added value can be adopted both in the private and public sectors and should be an active topic at any team or department meeting.

Obvious items to look at:

- Increasing sales
- Reducing costs—introduction of a creative ideas scheme
- Doing more with less resource
- Process re-engineering by section or department
- Managing noncertified absence
- Incentives for delivering budgets under budget

- Reducing training time (time away from work)
- Introducing mentors for informal coaching and knowledge enhancement
- Challenge all existing processes—are they current and needed?
- Introduce schemes that are directly aligned to promote productivity for talented employees
- Investigate and implement AI processes and, if appropriate, the use of robotics
- Examine the actual value of training and its direct relationship with organizational objectives

As a leader, one of the six elements that are essential here is:

Leadership skill 4. Great leaders recognize that communication takes time, and that you can't correct the past.

Communicate constantly—especially to your team.

A great way of motivating and getting the best from others is constant communication. In the west, the worst day for productivity is a Monday. So, why not start the week with a *quick* five-minute briefing right at the start of the day?

As a leader, it is up to you to set the tone quickly; no more than five minutes of upbeat briefing on the key targets for the week ahead. This is a great way to get everyone energized and into productive work mode. When doing this briefing, remember to:

- Make sure you speak to each individual before you start
- Hit the key targets for the week
- Don't talk about problems; focus on the future week, not the past
- End the briefing on a high note

There are many motivational theories about leadership. From experience, the one that works the best in today's fast-moving world for inspirational leaders is MBWA—management by walking about. It's always important to show an interest in all your staff and, wherever possible, give them positive feedback and encouragement. This is the opposite of how a manager would operate, who will often take great pleasure in pointing out people's failures and weaknesses. This is not the way to get things done in today's working and rapidly changing environment and with talented people.

When we are looking at changing the way we do things and getting people to come up with suggestions and new ideas, they will only do that if they get encouragement, and they are working in an environment that supports change. This is the environment the leader can create at *any* level in the organization.

When moving to set up departments as value-added centers, you need results and people who are not afraid to suggest changes or challenge the existing way things are done.

Just look at how electric cars have revolutionized the car industry in just a few years; dare to be different.

CHAPTER 4

Performance Appraisals That Matter

Traditional Appraisal System and the Cost of Achieving Very Little

Performance appraisal is one of the biggest human resources (HR) processes in most companies. Yet, for such a necessary process involving every employee, its cost is rarely challenged. The other question rarely explored is, does it work? Does performance appraisal do what it's supposed to do? According to Gallup, *only 14 percent of employees strongly agree their performance reviews inspire them to improve.*

In other words, if performance reviews were a drug, they would not meet FDA approval for efficacy.

For most organizations, the performance review is simply assumed to be "the right thing to do." That's how we're supposed to determine pay and establish accountability, right?

But in recent years, many business leaders have asked themselves, "Why do we do this in the first place?" Are our performance reviews really helping us get the most out of our people and engage them?

When organizations put their performance management system under a microscope, the answer is a resounding "NO." It does not equip, inspire, and improve performance. It is not the best system for determining pay and promotion.

And it costs organizations a lot of money—as much as $2.4 million to $35 million a year in lost working hours for an organization of 10,000 employees to take part in performance evaluations—with very little to show for it.

Does that mean organizations should throw out their performance reviews altogether and replace them with something new? And if so, what?

Work with Stanford University and Gallup's analytics—here's what we have learned:

- Performance reviews in most organizations are so bad that they do more harm than good.
- Traditional performance reviews and approaches to feedback are often so bad that they *actually make performance worse about one-third of the time.*

If traditional performance appraisal worked every year, productivity would rise. There should be a correlation between performance appraisal (productivity) and reduced employee numbers due to greater productivity within the organization.

Who Has the Responsibility for Performance Appraisal?

If you decouple measurable output from performance appraisal, then most HR professionals put their hands up to owning the process.

However, once the term measurement output is mentioned, the responsibility for the process and the outcome seems to transfer quickly to line management.

With performance appraisal being the single most significant tool for objective setting and performance measurement, how can it degenerate so quickly into an organizational orphan?

In the vast number of performance appraisal systems that are in place, it's inconceivable that so much can be spent on a process that delivers so little yet is still viewed as the best practice.

This is due to a common myth that best practice must always produce best practice results. If it is the best practice, then perhaps any HR bonus should be calculated on added value measurable output from the system.

As the process is clearly a shared responsibility with the line management, the output must form the basis of a shared key performance indicator.

Before you sign up for this being a good idea, you need to read on and see what is involved in getting benefits from this system.

A Severe Defect in Most Appraisal Systems

The operating fault of most current systems lies not just with the process and lack of accountability for bottom-line results but with a far more straightforward issue, an issue that is cheap, quick, and easy to remedy.

After speaking with over 1,000 HR professionals worldwide from a broad spectrum of industries, it is evident that the focus of appraisal makes positive, measurable outcomes impossible in most cases.

The consensus seems to be that once the appraisal system is installed, after the first year, a pattern of how the appraisal runs becomes evident. The actual time spent doing the appraisal seems to vary within plus or minus 15 minutes, the mean tending to be one hour in duration. What is of great interest is how that time is used.

It seems that most of the appraisal time is spent reviewing the previous year. In fact, the figure quoted amounts to a massive 80 percent. That's 80 percent looking back: on performance against objectives, identifying training needs and other factors that should not be discussed at a performance appraisal. We term this "the car rear view mirror effect."

The fault with this approach is that *nothing* can be done about the past or past performance. What's past is history; nothing will change what's already happened. If there are any lessons to be learned from failed objectives, then these should have been sorted out long before appraisal time.

The only thing we can plan for and be successful with is the future. This obsession with the previous year's past performance and activities is the single biggest reason for appraisals failing.

The rearview mirror approach is incompatible with today's fast-moving dynamic leadership approach.

With such a strong *past* focus, it leaves only 20 percent of the time of the appraisal left for future direction. It's not surprising that objectives are poorly set, and little, if any, actual performance measurement is planned or takes place. Because of this, managers are unwittingly setting their staff up for ongoing *failure*. This effect of setting employees up to fail is real and costly. Training is then identified based on failure or weaknesses.

When the employee fails, the feeling of failure, or a job not well done, pushes motivation down and hangs like a shadow of doom till the next appraisal, so training (usually the cure-all solution) is prescribed based on a failure that happened probably nine months before the appraisal.

Training then identified at appraisal goes through the system, which can be six months before it takes place.

To recap, in this example, a total of 15 months of elapsed time has been taken to rectify a past mistake or shortfall and provide a solution, in this case, training. This retrospective approach to appraisal makes no business sense and could easily be avoided by taking a different approach. HR managers, leaders, and certainly managing directors seem unaware of the actual cost of an appraisal system.

The Actual Cost of the Appraisal

If the appraisal is the most critical goal-setting tool an organization has, then we must be confident that it will yield a good return on investment and add value. So let's examine the appraisal cost for a company employing 3,000 people with an average employee unit cost of $46.00 per hour.

For each appraisal:

Appraiser's time preparing 0.5 hours × $46	$23.00
Appraisee's time preparing 0.5 hours × $46	$23.00
Appraisal time for Appraiser 1 × $46	$46.00
Appraisal time for Appraiser 1 × $46	$46.00
After the appraisal—completing documentation appraiser 0.5 hours × $46	$23.00
After the appraisal—talking and reflecting appraiser 0.5 hours × $46	$23.00
HR processing time for each appraisal 0.5 hours × $46	$23.00
Subtotal	$207.00
3,000 Employees × $207	$621,000.00

In addition, it would be fair to add the cost of misdirected training identified from the appraisal. This could be as high as 70 percent of the training budget—the cost of which would need to be added to the calculation.

In our example, we have a cost to the business of $621,000—to get just a simple return on investment; we need to get each year $621,000 of

Dr. Tony Miller's Formula for Organizational Change 2023/2024

FORMULA 1. Pearsons moment correlation for two data comparisons e.g., Age vs. productivity

$$r = \dfrac{\sum XY - \dfrac{(\sum X)\cdot(\sum Y)}{N}}{\sqrt{\left[\sum X^2 - \dfrac{(\sum X)^2}{N}\right]\cdot\left[\sum Y^2 - \dfrac{(\sum Y)^2}{N}\right]}}$$

FORMULA 2. Reliability (attendance) index

$S^1 \times S^2 \times D = BI > software = R\%$

S^1 is the spell of absence

S^2 is the spell of absence

D is the duration of the absence

BI is the Bradford Index (as modelled)

R is the reliability score based on a 1-100 scale

FORMULA 3. LSI Labor stability index

$\dfrac{\text{Number with more than one year's service now}}{\text{Total employed one year ago}} \times 100 = LSI$

FORMULA 4. How to right size your organization prior to A.I.

Full worked example provided

FORMULA 5. ESUC. Unit cost for any employee per day (divide by 8 for hourly rate)

Part 1
Total salary cost including all allowances x 2 = X

Total staff employed

Part 2 $\dfrac{X}{PWD}$ = ESUC

FORMULA 6. How much does appraisal cost?

Cost of performance appraisal (if you use 360 degree appraisal, multiply the end figure x 3) TH x TE x ESUC = annual cost of yearly appraisal

Where TH is the total hours spent, including, all processing time

TE is the total number of employees
ESUC is the unit cost per hour of each employee

FORMULA 7. The value of re-engineering a process

Cost of old process E - e is the cost of new process (plus change costs) = added value created per year

FORMULA 8. HR and training ROI

AV (actual business value created in one year) – total cost of activity = added value (or loss)

FORMULA 9. How many people do you need to run the organization?

Total staff employed x PWD – (sickness days training days and unauthorized absence) = Man days needed to run the organization

FORMULA 10. Calculating prime working days PWD

Number of days in the year 365 – (Public Holidays 10 + Weekends 104 + Annual Leave 25) = PWD 226

Figure 4.1 Formulas for organizational efficiency—formula 4

measurable bottom-line benefits just to cover the essential cost of the process. Can your appraisal system deliver this type of performance?

If you go beyond return on investment to seek added value, it would be reasonable to expect to see a 20 percent added value each year. In other words, each year the system is in place, we should expect to see minimum measurable benefits of $745,200.

If you are using 360-degree appraisal, then the cost of the process is massively increased and almost impossible to justify financially.

Leaders—A New Approach to Setting Performance Goals—Worked Example

Most organizations still follow slavishly the setting of specific, measurable, attainable, realistic, and timely (SMART) objectives.

SMART goals were developed by George Doran, Arthur Miller, and James Cunningham in their 1981 article There's a S.M.A.R.T. way to write management goals and objectives. It's great having a convenient acronym, but is it appropriate in today's business world? You can try this for yourself: get a group of managers together and ask them to write a SMART objective, it will take them ages, and in the end, it's doubtful if it will be logical and clear.

Setting clear objectives is very different for talented employees, so a different approach is needed.

Beyond SMART Objectives

The author designed the *Triple W objective setting*. Recognizing that leaders, managers, and supervisors did not apply SMART objectives, he used knowledge from his strategic mapping process to come up with a triple W objective setting. This methodology is ideal for translating strategic plans into action for large projects. If used at performance appraisal, the results are simply outstanding.

The Basic Concept—for Performance Appraisal

In the rapidly changing world we live in, the consensus is that successful organizations have moved quickly to the employment of talented people.

The advantage of talented people is that they are swift to work out how to do things and require little, if any, day-to-day management. This is the complete opposite of poor performers—bozos—bozos need to be told everything in minute detail, repeatedly. For a talent-focused current organization, the way objectives are set is essential. This triple W system requires the appraiser to set the *What*, *Why*, and *When* for the critical performance appraisal objectives. The talented person is then required to work out *how* best to do it. This builds a lot of commitment and ownership relating to the objective(s) set.

Although initially it looks like a lot of work, its standard format is not that hard to get to grips with. It can also be used for several other applications, including running big projects.

The Process

The first W is the what, what is it that needs to be done, or what is it that needs doing. This needs to be spelt out so that it's clear to understand.

Example of old method:

To improve productivity in the back office by 20 percent this year (that's before the triple W process).

What is required? New style.

- To increase the number of case files dealt with by 20 percent a month, that's 50 extra, 600 extra in a year.
- The work is to be locked into a project program on our Microsoft Office management system showing all the deliverables, dates, and number of extra files processed—the exact numbers to be shown for each month.

Why? Without the why, the person doing the objective will never fully understand the context of their objective and why; if they have this information, they may be able to produce a better way of doing it.

- For our organization to be competitive, we must increase our volume without incurring extra costs, such as more HR.
- The timing will be crucial as the sales force have concrete targets to achieve. This will directly affect our workload commencing

on October 1 this year, 2023. Everyone should be aware that
this is a priority as it is a critical element of our strategy.

When? It is critical here to be specific. Don't just give an end date.
Anyone who has managed projects will tell you that that's asking for slippage. So, take time to break the objective into manageable chunks. Dates
given should be by day, month, and year. When figures are involved, try
not to use percentages but exact numbers—this will avoid confusion or
misunderstanding.

This objective fits in with the department's strategy for continuous
improvement and innovation by demonstrating its efficiency improvements over the next five years.

- The plan for achieving this is required for outline approval by
  April 2, 2024. Then it must be agreed upon and approved by
  May 1, 2024.
- The first batch increase is needed by October 1, 2024
  (50 files), and the total objective is to be completed showing
  the 600 extra files by May 1, 2025.

One of the greatest assists to performance improvement is any business
using this system to ensure things get done on time and within budget.

Leaders and supervisors only require a short but focused piece of
training to be able to do this—remember, there is a vast difference
between the managers saying they can do it and the reality of well-
written objectives.

You may be wondering in the triple W objective method, why there
is no explanation of *how to do it*. With today's workforce, talented people
are bright enough to work this out themselves or to find out. If they take
the objective on board and work out how to do it, they will be more com-
mitted and accountable for the outcome as it's their idea. This simple but
effective approach does produce results and, more importantly, gets a lot
more commitment to action.

It's essential to give up the notion that people will automatically
improve or that performance/competency problems will sort themselves
out. This just does not happen in today's business world; therefore, quick
action that is helpful, effective, and decisive is required.

Get into a productivity-focused mode as a state of mind, a way of thinking things through. Always surround yourself with good people and carry this process through in all your recruitment efforts.

Performance is our key tool: it's not just getting people to work harder or smarter—we have a genuine job to do in ensuring leaders have the right tools and processes to make this happen. We also should seek out and destroy any processes or practices that take energy away from people. The late Peter Drucker summed up this approach very nicely when he said, "Would the roof cave in if we completely stopped doing this?" Often, we seem to have processes that don't add value but do absorb a lot of time and effort. A good example is the vacation process. You either have a vacation entitlement or you don't. Leave it for the individual to agree with their colleagues when to take the vacation; there is no need for several people in the company to record it. In one company, the finance department was the approver of everyone's vacation!

Background to Strategic Action Plans—Full Example as Used for Performance Appraisal Objective Setting

In this example, we can see how the appraising officer has set objectives for one of his staff. Creating a strategic action plan (SAP) to ensure that appraisal objectives are well defined, focused, and, most importantly, meet organizational requirements. Using SAPs ensures and covers:

- What is to be achieved
- What will be covered
- A plan of how and when each item is to be delivered
- Risks that might be associated with the delivery
- Dependencies—whom are you dependent upon to make things happen

An essential aspect of the document is that it is in a standard format and needs approval before and after delivery, ensuring that the end customer, in this case, the appraiser or sponsor, gets precisely what they expect.

Timing—A first cut of the SAP is to be ready by …
Sponsor—The customer/sponsor for each of the SAPs (that is you). The appraiser.

Methodology—Initially, the appraisee will produce their plans and timelines.

Help with the construction of the plans can be sought from …

It is essential here that the appraiser does not end up working out the HOW for the appraisee. That's the appraisee's job.

When completing the SAP, it is essential to stick to a standard methodology as all SAPs may need to be integrated eventually.

Front Cover

- Quality plan for *Objective name*
- Appraisee
- Version
- Version date
- Date approved

(Note: The version numbers should be in decimal points until approval. When this is determined, it becomes Version 1.)

Scope

What is the objective going to achieve, what will be covered, and also, what is excluded?

Deliverables

Each key objective will have many tasks, which together provide the components for the total objective. Each manageable task or group of tasks will make up one of the objective deliverables. In this section of the Quality Plan, all of the deliverables must be identified. If you have a team of people working on objectives, you will need to assign specific deliverables to the appropriate person.

Plan

The deliverables need to be translated into timelines so that the SAP can be tracked together with all the other plans and activities.

Risks

As with any key, new objective, there may be risks that, unless addressed, will adversely affect either the quality or timeliness of the objective. These need to be identified so that they can be addressed at an early stage.

Dependencies

Specific areas of your objective may depend on other people in the organization helping you. There may be a particular action needed before you can action specific critical tasks—these need to be included in the plan.

Sign-On

The appraiser will sign the SAP plans. This will happen when they are sure that all the elements are in place and that the complete plans provide the solution.

Sign-Off

Once the project is complete, the appraiser will sign off the documentation only when all the deliverables have been delivered to the agreed specification.

SAP—Example completed by the designed person Tom Smith following his appraisal. This is Tom's first-cut attempt.

Training needed for new working procedures and software: Designated person Tom Smith, Training Manager

Version.10

Version date 10-22-23

Date approved _____

Scope

To develop, test, and deliver a training program for new loan counselors, processors, their team leaders, and company direct managers; to create corporate awareness through the training of company customer suppliers and their staff.

This training program will be directed toward four major product areas:

- 30/15-year fixed conforming loans (and all other Desktop Originator products)
- 30/15-year federal housing administration (FHA) loans
- 3.30/15-year veterans affairs (VA) loans
- Equity lines of credit

Excluded from this SAP is the training of support personnel. A training program for these positions may be developed at a later time, depending on the needs yet to be determined.

Deliverables

The overall objective is to produce a training program that will train existing and new loan counselors, loan processors, and their leaders to staff the best call center in the world.

1. Design and build a training facility with the following attributes:
   a. Thirteen workstations—12 for trainees and 1 for the instructor. Workstations will be identical to workstations used in the workplace. In the call center, both in hardware and software, but under no circumstances are they able to access the call center programs. (Exact specifications to be provided by the system's SAP.) Also, some of the high-tech items will be required to enhance the training.
   b. The training facility needs an open area in addition to the workstation area to facilitate noncomputer group training. MIS 7-25-2023.
2. Record existing loan counselor/customer conversations for review by performance advantage. RE 5-23-2023.
3. Complete a need analysis to define some training blocks' requirements. As of this time, the projected training blocks would be as follows:
   a. Organizational culture and team building
   b. Relationship selling

    c. Product knowledge for 30-year fixed conforming loans and all other Desktop Originator products

    d. Telephone usage and predictive language

    e. Team leadership and coaching techniques

    f. Putting it all together, "One day in the life of a call center." RE 5-23-2023.

4. Complete a need analysis to define the requirements of the software training blocks. As of this time, the projected training blocks would be as follows:

    a. Use of Point Software

    b. Use of Desktop Originator software

    c. Use of Loan Prospector software

    d. Help/script pop-up screen utilization

    e. Product underwriting guidelines RE 7-12-2023

5. Set up terms of reference (e.g., measurement requirements)

    a. Total calls versus total sales

    b. Letters of praise

    c. Phone matrix

    d. Competency matrix

    e. Referrals RE 6-6-2023

    f. Define core skills (e.g., Point software, Desktop Originator software, and Loan Prospector software)

    Telephone usage and predictive language, accuracy of documentation, product knowledge RE 6-27-2023.

    g. Investigate the use of Brightware software for use in the Service Center. RE 7-3-2023.

    h. Develop a total training program with specific objectives and phases to ensure that, after training, the loan counselors, loan processors, and their leaders and managers will obtain a basic designated performance level based on the terms of reference and core skills. RE 7-25-2023.

    i. Develop lesson plans and a testing program to cover the content developed in the training program. RE 8-8-2023.

    j. Test the training program in a remedial mode using the existing staff. RE 8-15-2023.

k. Revise the training program based on feedback received from the existing staff. RE 8-29-2023.

l. Test the revised training program using the appropriate people. RE 8-21-2023.

m. Recruit the first class of 12 trainees. RE 9-4-2023.

n. Train the first group of potential team leaders. RE 9-19-2023.

o. Train the first class of 12 trainees with the participation of the team leaders. RE 9-26-2023. Develop training modules for other product areas, FHA, VA, and equity lines. RE 10-5-2023.

p. Use portions of the training mentioned above modules to articulate the vision of organizational requirements to managers, customer suppliers, and their staff.

q. Implement the use of video, multimedia, and other high-tech training enhancements.

r. Train other individuals to deliver training when needed.

Risks

1. An adequate training facility may not be available, significantly reducing training efficiency.

2. Point software may be so primitive and user-unfriendly that it intimidates and discourages the new trainee, making it impossible to achieve the desired goals.

3. The technology group is unable or unwilling to provide the support necessary to set up help/script pop-up screens in the required time frame.

4. The technology group is unable or unwilling to provide the support necessary to set up product underwriting criteria screens in the required time frame.

5. There are not enough qualified potential team leaders.

Dependencies

1. We need the technology group to approve specifications and set up the computer portion of the training facility. By (work in hand).

2. Need the technology group to design and implement help/script pop-up screens and timing flags (wake-up calls). (Work in hand).

3. Need the technology group to design and implement underwriting criteria screens. (Work in hand).

4. Need the technology group to set up a phone system to record existing loan counselor/customer conversations to be used in the predictive language study. 4.1.2023.

5. Need performance advantage to analyze existing loan counselor/customer conversations using predictive language techniques to develop the content for help/script pop-up screens. 4.1.2023.

6. Need Dr. Tony to provide recruitment policy and procedures. 5.1.2023.

7. Need Dr. Tony to provide loan counselor and team leader salary and remuneration policy and procedures. 5.1.2023.

8. Need Nick to provide content for parts of the training. From 5.1.2023.

9. Need Ann Saunders to develop the content for product underwriting guideline screens. 5.1.2023.

10. Need Ann Saunders to provide product knowledge information. 5.1.2023.

11. Need Sara/Dr. Tony to provide Tom Smith with predictive language training. Before 4.1.2023.

12. Need Dr. Tony to give a cultural template for use in the development of the training program. Before 4.1.2023.

13. Need the CEO to provide the vision portion of the training at the beginning of each training session. 6.1.2023.

14. Need the team leaders to participate in the trainees' training. (Work in hand)

Approved by   Appraising officer
                     Jan Hanson   *Date*

When actioning appraisal objectives, the methodology shown in this chapter suits our purposes. We must often get things done through others in the organization, and sometimes those people do not work directly for us; the SAPs get everyone on the same page.

Some companies use SAPs at appraisal time and get the person being appraised to complete one for each objective they have been set. This produces excellent results and brings real commitment and buy-in from the employee.

This example may seem complicated. Remember Tom Smith is the training manager and is thoroughly familiar with the existing process. He is the ideal person to carry out this objective as part of his objectives from performance appraisal. The SAP you have seen is Tom's first attempt at getting his plan of HOW to do it ready.

Use the FACE Technique

This methodology can be used as a check on many things at work; FACE stands for

*F*AST is the new method or creative idea Fast? What is the saving in time or money? Will it give us a real edge?

*A*CCURATE will this reduce errors? if so, how many and how much can we save?

*C*OST-effective Is this a benefit? Is it the best for our organization?

*E*ASY Is the system, process, or innovation easy to use—for the user? Is it in line with our future direction?

It's good to think about this, particularly when working out the HOW to do it for performance objectives or when instigating new procedures and processes.

Linking Performance Appraisal Into the Bigger Picture

What should performance appraisal provide:

- Realistic setting and achieving of organizations goals
- A motivational tool—success breeds success
- A tool to identify training, if needed, based on future needs, not past performance
- An accurate feed into a hopper bonus scheme
- A key process to measurably increase productivity and organizational efficiency
- A critical process for analysis and predictive forecasting for artificial intelligence (AI)

- A process that encourages people to grow and improve year on year
- A bond between the leader (appraiser) and their team—looking to the future to achieve organizational objectives

Is Appraisal a Motivational Tool?

Is appraisal a motivational tool? Just ask yourself, will employees be more motivated by failure—the old rear mirror approach, or will employees be more motivated by success in an environment that breeds success; the forward success-driven approach?

Motivational success through appraisal can be measured. Do some statistical analysis such as measuring sickness levels before adopting the new approach and then examining the sickness levels after. Also, look at staff turnover both before the adoption of the new system and after. Staff satisfaction surveys are also a useful indicator.

The term motivation is often wrapped in with the benefits of appraisal.

If the appraisal is an essential motivational tool, then management needs help to get the new approach right.

Organizational Benefits

Changing the focus of appraisal is a case of everything to gain and little to lose.

In AI terms, performance appraisal is correctly focused and is the hub for most organizational activities.

Some of the organizational benefits that should be seen include projects delivered on time and within budget, reduced absenteeism levels, improved staff morale, reduced training budget, a more agile organization, and lower staff turnover in the long term.

The process will clearly identify poor-performing managers, supervisors, and employees and will enable a definite and measurable impact on the bottom line to be seen.

Although this might seem appropriate only to the private sector, many of the benefits mentioned do map very nicely into the public sector. There should also be a change in the way appraisal is viewed, as this gives a clear indicator that it is adding value by using business skills to enhance business performance.

Very shortly, AI will measure all activities and determine which produce performance results (see Figure 4.2). The performance appraisal system will also check how managers rate their staff and precisely how much training they get. If staff are identified for lots of training—was that because they were not competent? If so, was that due to poor recruitment? The impact would be that they would not qualify for any bonus as their competency score would be below the preset standard. Refer to Figure 2.2 Productivity dashboard, referred to in Chapter 2.

The most crucial factor in any appraisal system is to improve productivity. AI will constantly monitor the relationships between performance appraisal scores and the benefits the organization has seen. This may seem very obvious, but it's seldom done as many organizations view performance appraisal as an unreliable tool—but continue year after year to use it.

The appraisal should be a big motivator, a time to say *well done* for the previous year's work and an exciting time to look to the future. This can be viewed either by AI or workforce planners; motivated staff tend to have less time off work. That can be measured as an improvement that has a direct financial impact on the organization. Also, motivated staff are less likely to leave the organization; again, another value-added activity. A word of caution about turnover. The people you want to retain are the talented group and the top 40 percent of average performers. The people you want to leave are, of course, your poor performers.

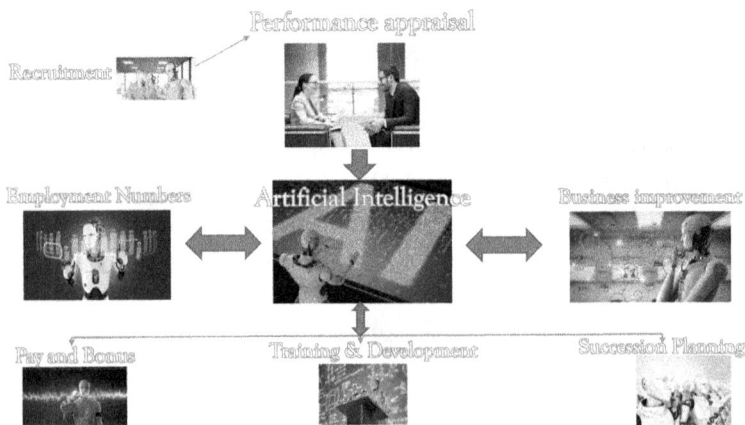

Figure 4.2 Where AI fits

CHAPTER 5

The Future of Remote Work

Remote Working—The Benefits and Issues for Employees

Very little good has come from the COVID-19 epidemic. It has, however, created a new world of work. Despite years of managers saying, "if people work from home or remotely, they won't do any work," the reverse has been the case. Many case studies have shown productivity increases, which can be described as substantial. According to a recent McKinsey *American Opportunity* report, nearly 90 percent of the people surveyed said, if offered, they would accept a flexible work option. This finding was consistent across the demographics among the 25,000 Americans polled. In the United States, almost 60 percent of people currently work from home at least one day a week, with 35 percent working from home full time.

A recent study just published by Birmingham University shows that even managers can see improved productivity can come from remote working. Birmingham University has found that managers developed a more positive outlook on the benefits of remote and flexible working since the COVID-19 outbreak and agreed that working from home improves employee concentration; 59.5 percent agreed that it increases productivity, and 62.8 percent agreed that it increases motivation. Furthermore, an even larger proportion of managers, 76.5 percent, believes that flexible working generally increases productivity. Importantly, the study also found that line managers were more likely to see flexible working as a performance-enhancing tool (71.2 percent) than senior management (65.6 percent). This highlights the importance of educating senior management on the benefits of flexible working and the positive impact it can have on employee performance (Entrepreneur Gleb Tsipursky, January 14, 2023).

With child care issues, concerns about COVID-19 resurgences, and other potential health hazards like Monkeypox, burnout, and the savings on gas achieved by not having to commute, a flexible work model provides the answer to achieving a greater work–life balance.

Other research in America, which you may find interesting, has shown working from home is a relatively new experience for a majority of workers with jobs that can be done remotely—57 percent say they rarely or never worked remotely prior to the coronavirus outbreak. For those who have switched to homeworking, their work lives have changed in some significant ways. On the plus side, most (64 percent) of those who are now working remotely at least some of the time but rarely or never did before the pandemic say it's easier now for them to balance work with their personal life: And many (44 percent) say working from home has made it easier for them to get their work done and meet deadlines, while very few (10 percent) say it's been harder to do this. At the same time, 60 percent say they feel less connected to their co-workers now. Most (72 percent) say working from home hasn't affected their ability to advance in their job.

So, what are the significant benefits of remote working for the employee?

Commuting

Most people have to commute to get to their place of work. In the UK, the capital London is a location used for the data given here:

- Time traveling to and from work daily 3.5 hours
- Cost of rail fare to and from London (average) per year £5,680.00 (U.S.$6,916.00)
- Cost of food and beverages while traveling and at work 226 PWD × £8.00 = £1,808 (U.S.$2,202)

For our commuter, the savings per year amounts to £7,488.00 (U.S.$9,118.00).

Time saved in a year (minimum) 3.5 hours × 226 PWD = 791 hours

Remote Working Where Situated?

For remote workers, the cost savings and time are very significant. Also, the quality of life is better, less stress and more time with the family and loved ones.

Remote working does not necessarily mean working from home. It could be in any remote location or a mixture of both—called hybrid working. A coffee shop, public library, a beach in Barbados, anywhere where you have the Internet and are productive when working. Although remote work has a great amount of flexibility today, surprisingly, the majority of remote workers (84 percent) work where they live. According to recent studies 2022/2023, remote workers feel that working from home improves their performance because of the convenience and the quieter work environment.

You need to be disciplined and get into a routine that works for you. A good strategy is to keep a daily log of how you spend your time. Record it in 30-minute slots. It will help keep you on track, and should you require it later, it will provide you with an accurate picture of how you have spent your time. This technique is used by most consultants, lawyers, and accountants who have to account for and bill their time to clients.

So, what type of person are you? Do you see yourself as someone who views the current situation of change as positive or negative?

You Can Live Where You Want to

Approximately five million workers *moved* between 2020 and 2022 because remote work made it possible. No longer connected with a physical office, many fully remote employees could keep their jobs and move closer to family, to a dream location, or to an *area with a lower cost of living*. (Maybe all three!) Just keep in mind that in some cases—like employers that want you to attend in-person meetings once a week—changing locations may not be ideal. You should also make sure to check that your organization can legally employ someone based in the state or country you're looking to move to (*The Muse*).

Typical Types and Their Views

Is your glass half empty (pessimist), or is your glass half full (optimist)?

A pessimist would view remote working as:

- Only a temporary measure, and I will be glad when things get back to normal.
- Resent having to use my own laptop and equipment.
- Be worried about making decisions without their manager to support them.
- See this situation as an encroachment on their family life.
- Worry about who will pay for the extra electricity used to recharge the laptop.

An optimist would view remote working as:

- Inevitable and a great chance to do things differently.
- No more commuting.
- I will save lots of money.
- A tremendous amount of flexibility.
- Perhaps I don't need a car anymore?
- It means immense freedom—I could work from anywhere or do something completely different.

One common theme among remote workers is that they can feel isolated. The universal use of Skype, WhatsApp, Microsoft Teams, or Sysco Webex means we can all be in touch with our work colleagues when needed.

Start-Up Opportunities

If you have ever thought of starting up your own business, there has never been a better time. Working patterns and people's needs have changed dramatically during the COVID-19 period. Everywhere you will see good deals on shops and office premises. All you need is a business opportunity that you see as an extension of what already exists or something completely new that will explore a new idea in a rapidly

A new start up – which direction to take?

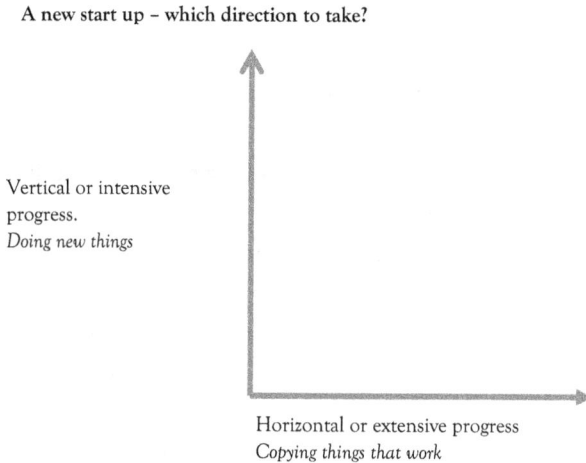

Vertical or intensive
progress.
Doing new things

Horizontal or extensive progress
Copying things that work

Figure 5.1 Which direction to take?

changing environment. In his book *Zero to One*, Peter Thiel explains
how the current business environment has opened up a range of new
opportunities. Of particular interest is his model (see Figure 5.1), which
helps you to focus on which direction to take.

The vertical line typically relates to technology in its many guises, but
this is not exclusive.

Match your thinking to the current environment, masses of change in
every aspect of our lives; do you have that unique idea(s) that could make
you the next Elon Musk?

Will Remote Working Make You Happier?

A new study found that the ability to work remotely is strongly linked to
happiness at work. In the study by Tracking Happiness, 12,455 employees were surveyed about their work conditions. A total of 65.1 percent
of respondents were male, and 34.5 percent were female. The location of
the respondents varied with 38.6 percent coming from North America,
36.1 percent coming from Asia, 19.5 percent from South America, and
5.1 percent from Europe.

The survey respondents were asked, "If you look at your work,
how would you rate your happiness on a scale from one to ten?" and
"How much of your work is currently done remotely or from home?"

Key findings of the study include:

- The ability to work remotely increases employee happiness by as much as 20 percent.
- Millennials are happiest when working remotely. That is Generations Y and Z.
- Returning to office-based work after the pandemic reduces employee happiness.
- Employee happiness decreases as commute times increase.
- Happiness at work is significantly correlated to overall life happiness.

Remote Working and Your Body Clock

Remote working allows you to work in harmony with your body; it's a Lark and Owl syndrome. This is referred to as our biological clock works on its own—a roughly 24-hour cycle called a circadian rhythm—and the environment regulates the clock so that we go to sleep and wake up on the same schedule. Larks are the early risers who normally don't work late into the night. Owls are best later in the day. Remote working gives you the opportunity to work when it's best for your body clock, therefore getting the best out of yourself and helping yourself to be more in harmony with your body. Learn to recognize what time of the day works for what type of activity for you specifically, and then schedule your day accordingly. To get the most of your days, consider napping at the appropriate time. Also, to keep your internal clock healthy and aligned, have a routine. Get to bed and wake up at the regular time as much as possible, including weekends. Routine aligned with your circadian rhythms will work miracles.

How Personality Profiling Can Help With Remote Worker Selection

WARNING: Not everyone is suited for home working. When employers interview or screen people who will be remote workers, it's very important to examine their personality profile. With that information, we can significantly reduce the risk of trying to put a square peg into a round hole.

We will look again at the McCrae and Costa big five profiler OCEAN as explained in Chapter 1.

People who are suited for home working are likely to have a profile shown on the chart.

- Medium score in O, openness
- High C, conscientiousness
- Mid-range in E, extraversion
- Average and higher in A, agreeableness
- Average to low score in N, neuroticism

Many big companies use profiling as the gateway to an interview; Google profiling has worked exceptionally well for them, as it has also done for Facebook. The low scorers in openness are likely to sound like the pessimist—glass half empty, and it may be very difficult for them to move to a different way of working. Currently, people have been moved to remote working without profiling; this means many of those people will not be good employees in that situation. It's not that remote working

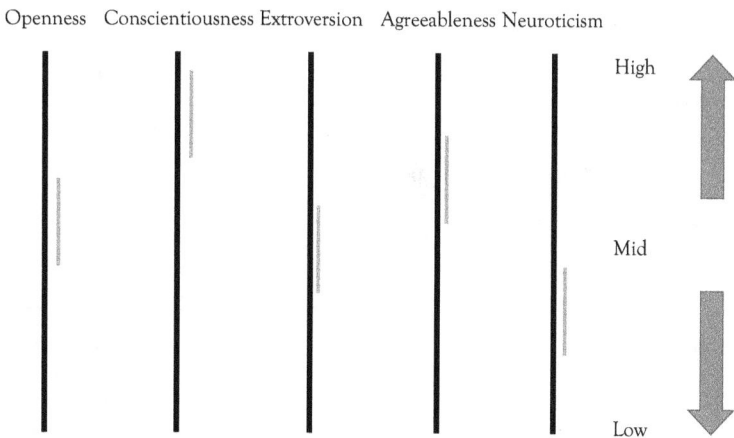

Openness   Conscientiousness   Extroversion   Agreeableness   Neuroticism

High

Mid

Low

Figure 5.2 OCEAN

does not work; rather, the wrong type of person has been allowed to be a remote worker.

To recap the big five—these are the brief descriptors:

1. The first observable trait in the OCEAN personality traits model is *openness* to experience, which describes an individual's creativity, curiosity, and culture. Openness to experience explores an individual's willingness to try new things and ability to think outside the box when tasked with something difficult. High scores are described as curious, creative, imaginative, and unconventional. Participants with a low score are considered more predictable and resistant to change.

2. The personality trait of *conscientiousness* relates to an individual's hardworking nature, organization, and dependability. Individuals with a high conscientiousness rating have high competence, good organization, strong self-discipline, and a drive to obtain recognition or achievement.

3. *Extraversion* is the personality trait used to comment on an individual's sociability, assertiveness, and outgoing nature toward others. It can be measured by observing an individual's energy during and after social interaction and confidence while speaking to others. Low scores on the scale are known as introverts.

4. *Agreeableness* refers to how people tend to treat relationships with others. Unlike extraversion, which consists of the pursuit of relationships, agreeableness focuses on people's orientation and interactions with others.

   Those low in agreeableness may be perceived as suspicious, manipulative, and uncooperative.

5. *Neuroticism*

   Those who score high on neuroticism often feel anxious, insecure, and self-pitying. They are often perceived as moody and irritable. They are prone to excessive sadness and low self-esteem.

   To view your profile, you could go to Cambridge Universities website, Apply Magic sauce and just download it—at the moment, it's free! https://applymagicsauce.com/demo

The Massive Value Remote Workers Can Give to an Organization

Remote workers need new contracts of employment; in such a contract, it needs to be very clear what type of remote working the employer is talking about:

- Remote working, where the employer expects the employee to be available, say 40 hours a week at home or a remote location carrying out 40 hours of work in line with the general working hours of their organization.

- Flexible remote working, where the employee does their work over a 24-hour—seven days a week span, but 40 hours needs to be worked. This gives employees the greatest flexibility. Flexibility empowers workers as it provides them with autonomy over their work lives. A flexible work model offers employees the trust to curate their own schedules. They can decide when and where they want to work. With management buy-in, the employee can create their own schedule, along with input from their team leaders, without fear of being reprimanded for carving time out to see their children's school plays or visiting the doctor. A person may decide to go to office five days a week and then work remotely for the rest of the month. By enabling people to design their own schedules, it's highly likely that they'll be happier and more productive.

- Hybrid working, where the employee works in the office for X days and remotely for the remainder. The downside of this is the old-style managers will still want to be employed to keep their old status quo.

- People crave the opportunity to be trusted to do their best work, as a cookie-cutter forced program may not align with their needs and hamper their productivity. In a separate study conducted by the Pew Research Center from this year, 48 percent of respondents with a child 18 years or younger left their jobs because of inadequate or nonexistent child care options. Nearly 40 percent of those surveyed said they quit because they were working too much. Unable to make their own hours, 45 percent of workers left their organizations due to a lack of flexibility. This should be a clear signal about how and where remote workers work and the type of leadership that will work best in this new working environment (Robinson 2022a).

Again, profiling is key here, and remember, home working will work best for 40 percent of the average employees and for the talented employees in the company. Poor performers will cause you a mass of problems if allowed to be remote workers.

Using Remote Workers Has Enormous Savings for the Employer

- Pay, for instance, you can pay remote workers less. When negotiating for pay deals, commuters always link demands to the increased costs of travel—it will no longer exist. For professionals, the cost of business clothing is also a significant factor.
- UYO, use your own. It's inconceivable in today's world that a remote worker won't have a laptop, cell phone, and access to a printer. The trend is UYO and not funded by the employer as it's a tool you need to fulfill your job requirements. The same applies to those asking for the organization to provide them with a home office or beach chair when working in Barbados. The sale of Apple laptops scored in 2021—due, I suspect, to the massive increase in remote working (Statista).
- Office space is a big issue. Companies have already reduced office space, look around any city, and you will see the evidence of a glut of vacant office space.

    Reuters (April 13, 2021) JP Morgan will need *significantly* less office space in coming years, as some staff at the investment bank shift permanently to part-time work at home. The bank is expected to need just 60 seats per 100 people, boss Jamie Dimon wrote in his annual shareholder letter.

HSBC announced it was reducing office space globally by 40 percent.

Nationwide Financial Services reported that post-COVID-19, 14,000 staff would not be returning to the branches to work (2021).

B.P. (March 8, 2021) announced that 25,000 of its workforce would work remotely at least two days a week.

Facebook (2020) reported by VERGE—Half of Facebook's staff to work from home within 10 years.

According to a property survey, as much as a fifth of office space in London and southeast England may not be required in the postpandemic world of work as employees spend less time at their desks.

- The new workplace flexibility is being offered to staff by their employers. It could leave office blocks empty across towns and cities, the real estate consultancy Lambert Smith Hampton (LSH) found in its latest office market report, as companies cut back on the amount of space they rent.

- In June 2022, *The Guardian* newspaper reported a 20 percent reduction in the office space needed by businesses. Compared with before, COVID-19, which represents about 26 m sq ft—equivalent to more than 15 times the amount of office space in the 50-story One Canada Square skyscraper in London's Canary Wharf, or more than double the entire stock of the reading office market.

  The desire for remote working is being driven, it seems, by the worker's costly fares and long commutes blamed as only one in 10 workers in capital (London) think full-time office return likely, reported *The Guardian* newspaper in June 2022.

  Office space, particularly in cities, is extremely expensive. Reducing office space enables organizations to reduce their operating costs significantly.

- With remote workers accounting for a significant proportion of the workforce, there is an immediate need to overhaul the structure of organizations and to ask the question, what role do managers and supervisors have now? Rightsizing and restructuring will give further significant organizational improvements. Now is the time for a new breed of leaders to emerge.

- *Productivity gains.* If you look at creditable research on remote workers, most published research shows a rise in productivity. Perhaps because today's workers don't need managers?

  According to the Airtasker study, which seems very much in line with other reports. Remote workers worked "1.4 more days every month or 16.8 more days yearly" than those working in an office. It would take less than an hour to work out using these figures how much total extra value home workers are giving the organization. You could then do another rightsizing, producing further organizational benefits. This was also reported in the *Harvard Business Review*.

The organizational benefits are massive, providing the flexibility to further invest in AI and other technologies. Those involved in work-force planning and organizational costing should know that the ESUC Employee Standard Unit Cost will decrease across the organization.

In Part 1 of the calculation, the multiplying factor is ×2. Remote workers (homeworkers) will reduce that cost to 1.5 or lower depending on how many remote workers the organization has (see Figure 5.3). Your ESUC will decrease so that your overall labor cost will be less due to your remote worker cost and efficiency.

Interesting Research Findings

1. *Airtasker* surveyed more than a 1,000 full-time employees about their productivity; more than half of the respondents worked from home. The survey's results bear a resemblance to those from Stanford University, indicating that remote workers put in more time compared to in-office workers.

2. Stanford University and Ctrip WFH Study Findings
   Perhaps the most prominent study exploring productivity and work-from-home arrangements is one conducted by researchers from Stanford University. The study *involved call center employees*

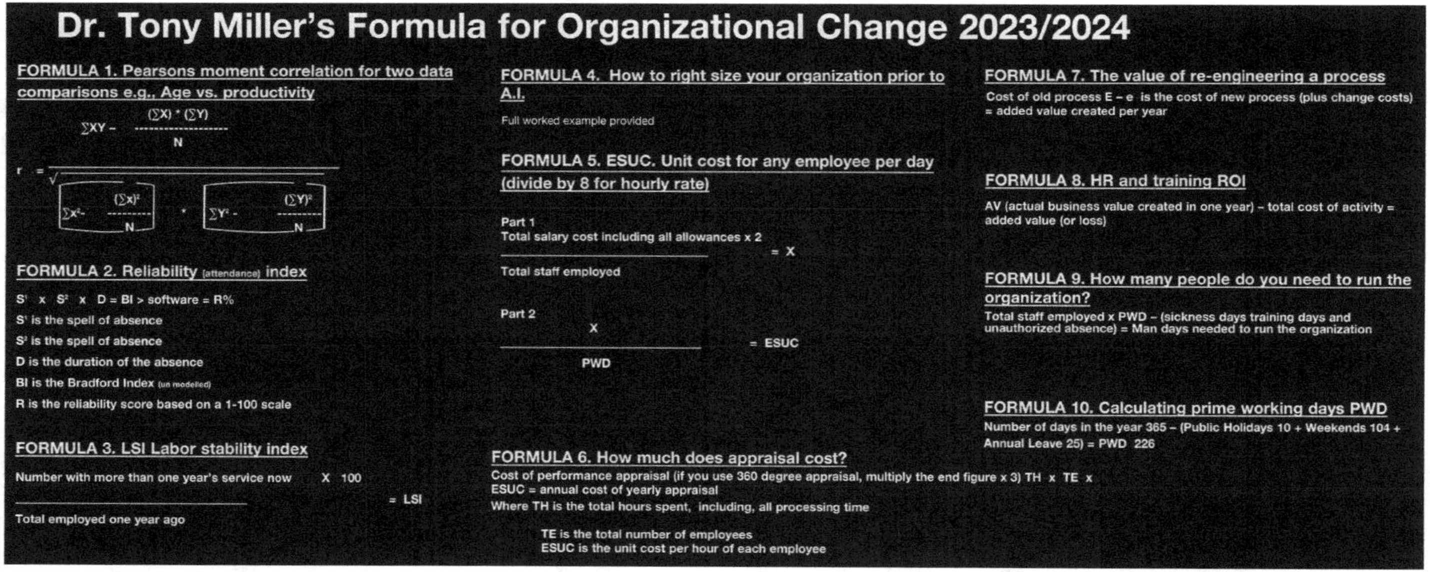

Dr. Tony Miller's Formula for Organizational Change 2023/2024

FORMULA 1. Pearsons moment correlation for two data comparisons e.g., Age vs. productivity

$$r = \dfrac{\Sigma XY - \dfrac{(\Sigma X) \cdot (\Sigma Y)}{N}}{\sqrt{\left[\Sigma X^2 - \dfrac{(\Sigma X)^2}{N}\right] \cdot \left[\Sigma Y^2 - \dfrac{(\Sigma Y)^2}{N}\right]}}$$

FORMULA 2. Reliability (attendance) index

$S^1 \times S^1 \times D = BI > \text{software} = R\%$

S^1 is the spell of absence

S^1 is the spell of absence

D is the duration of the absence

BI is the Bradford Index (as modified)

R is the reliability score based on a 1–100 scale

FORMULA 3. LSI Labor stability index

Number with more than one year's service now

_____ X 100   = LSI

Total employed one year ago

FORMULA 4. How to right size your organization prior to A.I.

Full worked example provided

FORMULA 5. ESUC. Unit cost for any employee per day (divide by 8 for hourly rate)

Part 1

Total salary cost including all allowances x 2   = X

Total staff employed

Part 2

X

_____ = ESUC

PWD

FORMULA 6. How much does appraisal cost?

Cost of performance appraisal (if you use 360 degree appraisal, multiply the end figure x 3)

ESUC = annual cost of yearly appraisal

Where TH is the total hours spent, including, all processing time

TE is the total number of employees.

ESUC is the unit cost per hour of each employee

FORMULA 7. The value of re-engineering a process

Cost of old process E – e is the cost of new process (plus change costs) = added value created per year

FORMULA 8. HR and training ROI

AV (actual business value created in one year) – total cost of activity = added value (or loss)

FORMULA 9. How many people do you need to run the organization?

Total staff employed x PWD – (sickness days training days and unauthorized absence) = Min days needed to run the organization

FORMULA 10. Calculating prime working days PWD

Number of days in the year 365 – (Public Holidays 10 + Weekends 104 + Annual Leave 25) = PWD 226

Figure 5.3 ESUC calculations (Calculation 5)

from Ctrip, a NASDAQ-listed Chinese travel agency with 16,000 employees. To conclude, the study used an experiment with a treatment group of work-from-home employees and a control group of their on-site counterparts.

This Ctrip study supports many common beliefs about the effects of WFH policies. For instance, the researchers found that home working resulted in a *13 percent performance increase*. Specifically, this performance increase was attributed to fewer breaks and sick days and a quieter, more convenient working environment. In the long run, the impact of home working on employee performance rose to 22 percent.

Moreover, this collaborative research effort between Stanford University and Ctrip found that home working improved work satisfaction. The treatment group reported a higher positive attitude and less exhaustion from work. Likewise, the treatment group had less than half the attrition rate (17 percent) of the control group (35 percent).

3. What Does the Scientific Data Show?

   To resolve the debate, it's time to go beyond subjective opinion and look at the objective science. David Powell, President of *Prodoscore*, said their data showed that if an employee was highly productive in-office, they'll be productive at home; if an employee slacked off at the office, they'll do the same a home. "After evaluating over 105 million data points from 30,000 U.S.-based Prodoscore users, we discovered a five per cent increase in productivity during the pandemic work from home period," he said. "Although, as we know, any variant of the COVID-19 virus is unpredictable, employee productivity is not" (Prodoscore).

4. A massive breakthrough. Managers finally realized and accepted that remote workers do improve productivity! The research was done by Birmingham University and reported in January 2023.

The Changes Needed for a Remote Working Culture

Remote working brings many advantages and some rather significant pitfalls for employers to be aware of. Very recently, some trade unions have started to say it's an employee's right to be able to do remote working. Shortly I can imagine this being extended to new mothers and other areas of the workforce. HR needs to be alert. It's the employer who makes the decision and decides the suitability of those best able to be remote workers depending on personality, the numbers involved, and in which areas of the business. All of this is a massive paradigm shift.

A definition of paradigm may be of use:

As there is such a massive change in the nature of work, employment contracts must be examined and quickly updated to reflect the paradigm shift in working practices. When you look up "paradigm" in the dictionary, you find it means "pattern" or "model."

A paradigm is a system of rules and regulations that does two things:

First, some of the rules set limits or establish boundaries—just like a pattern sets the edges.

Then, the rest of the rules offer you guidance on how to be successful by solving problems that exist inside those boundaries—in a sense, they offer you a model for problem-solving.

So a paradigm is a problem-solving system. And a paradigm shift is when you change from one set of rules to another.

Contract of employment. The employment contract provides the basis for either creating high productivity or generating many problems. Current employment law in Europe and the United States makes it very difficult to alter any aspect of their contractual agreement. The written word always takes precedence, so take care and get the best legal advice when setting up your contract templates. The expense will be well worth it in the long run. Also, you may want to show your lawyer this chapter as they will find the concepts of use when producing your agreements.

Employers may wish to consider working to *at will* or on short-term contracts during this massive change in employment and the way we work and where we work. Remote working could also be considered with an entire department, agreeing to a fixed salary for three years to provide the same service they offered as an in-house department. The group, for example, the purchasing department, would set themselves up as a unit but work off the premises. The unit would be independent of the organization but would bill for its services monthly. Suppose the purchasing unit had 10 people and one left. In that case, the unit may decide to run with nine people and divide the tenth person's salary among the remaining nine—an exciting possibility and thinking out-of-the-box approach.

Providing IT support for remote workers would need to be run and managed online. This would require a new approach to rapid response, which would be delivered remotely. Services will need to extend to 24-hour IT support, including weekends! IT support would need to match the hours and work patterns of the new breed of remote worker. ChatGPT 4 will reduce such dependencies significantly.

The problem group is as always going to be poor performers. Every effort needs to be made to remove them from the organization. If allowed to be remote workers, their productivity will drop for this group to almost zero. This group will not understand the rapidly changing world of work and will want managing, supervising, continuous training, and disproportional special attention.

In many organizations, managers have historically failed to address the issue of poor performers. There will never be an easy way to do this. Now is a golden opportunity to tackle this issue. Left to AI, it will do this faster than the blink of an eye.

The ongoing future of remote working will depend on many variables. One thing is for sure we will never go back to the world of work pre-2023.

Remote working is definitely growing as it's in most employees' best interest. Financially it's a massive cost saver for organizations. The big unknown is if organizations want employees back in the workplace—will it happen?

From information from reliable sources, employees are unlikely to return to existing work environments—even if directed (see Figure 5.4).

Not Everyone Is a Winner

Home working has had a dramatic effect on small businesses in cities. Primarily coffee and sandwich shops have been significantly adversely impacted by the remote working trend. The rail networks have seen a

The shape of future work

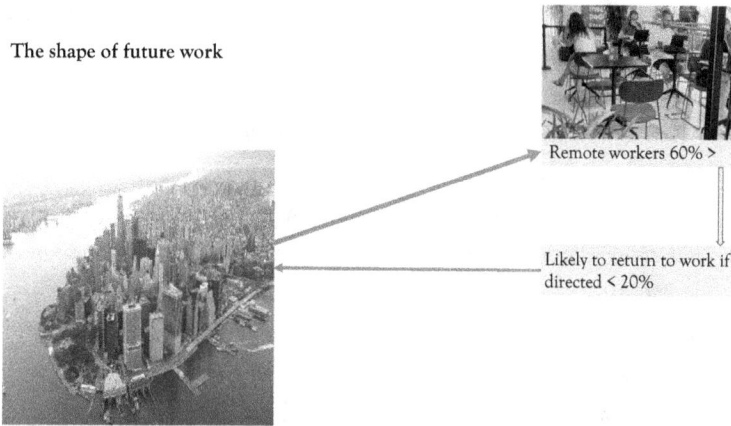

Remote workers 60% >

Likely to return to work if
directed < 20%

Figure 5.4 The shape of future work

massive reduction in commuters on a large scale. In the UK, rail income
has collapsed by 75 percent. The ghost trains carrying just a handful of
passengers became one of the emblems of the coronavirus pandemic in
the UK—with railwaymen and women on the frontline, keeping the
system running for essential workers. As this trend continues, I'm sure
we will see cuts in rail projects as they will be no longer financially viable.

Not Every Home Worker Can Be Trusted

Earlier, we mentioned about the need to profile those suitable to be
remote workers. Failure to do profile will lead to the abuse of the system
by poor performers and those with a low C (conscientiousness) on the
OCEAN personality inventory. Don't start writing masses of procedures
and checks to bring them in line; these are the people who were never
suited to remote working in the first place. The requirement of remote
workers (don't ever refer to them as home workers) needs to be clearly
spelt out in an employment contract fashioned by a legal employment
expert. It should also state the obvious, the minimum number of hours
to be *worked* in a week and exactly how that's to be recorded. Or just pay
remote workers for work done with no fixed hours at all.

Increasingly, employers are tracking remote working employees, a
popular software is *TimeCamp*. The following summary of an employee

who got caught out was reported by the *New York Independent* paper in January 2023:

> A *Woman ordered to repay employer $2,756 after computer software tracked her productivity*
>
> *The Civil Resolution Tribunal ultimately dismissed Karlee Besse's "just cause" claim, and ordered Besse to repay Reach CPA a total of $2,756.89 – including damages for time theft and additional costs – within 30 days. In a post-pandemic era of remote working, more companies have installed tracking software on workers' computers to ensure employees stay focused on work-related tasks while working from home. Reported Meredith Clark. New York Independent News Paper Saturday January 14, 2023.*

- 19% Convenience for having breaks
- 17% Quieter working environment
- 13% Easier to work when I'm not feeling well enough to commute
- 12% Feeling more positive toward the company

Figure 5.5 What remote workers like

CHAPTER 6

A New Way of Rewarding Success

Using Current Information to Formulate Equitable Big Reward Bonus Schemes

The new world of working and new leadership requires a significant rethink of how we pay and reward people. Also, meeting their expectations on what the world of work needs to be like. There is no universal formula that can be applied, and most of the new methods of rewards depend on what the talented employees want.

We have moved from telling talented employees what they will get to one of listening and providing them with what they expect for them to be able to produce at a very high level.

There are many motivators; no, this is not about old motivational theories but about what works today. The big issue is basic pay, bonus, and goodies. Basic pay has always got to be in the marketplace ballpark figure. The big difference can be made on the type of bonus scheme you have and how truthful you are on how it will work. The worst scenario is to have a structure of pay and rewards, which is very average.

Still, in many organizations, bonus systems are rigged. Two methods are used, the first is to say the maximum bonus we can pay is 10 percent. Then everyone believes that they will get a bonus only to be disappointed. Talented people will see it as an insult and make plans to leave. Poor performers will expect it and be outraged if they are excluded.

The second popular method is to offer bonuses based on meeting and exceeding your objectives. Then, at the end of the year, department heads are told that the bonus pot has been examined, that only a percentage of the staff can be eligible, and that any bonus will be subject to capping. In short, the company had no intention of paying out a substantial bonus to anyone. Regardless of how hard or how many objectives had been met! To say this is dishonest and underhanded is an understatement (see Figure 6.1). However, it is prevalent as it's shown as another organizational saving. Talented people will not get caught twice; they will leave. Staff will recognize they have been cheated and will be very cautious of management promises in future. Trust can then become an organizational issue.

So, what do talented people want? Having listened to truly talented people over several years, I have compiled a list of reoccurring comments I have heard and insights from some of the top world companies. Here are some of the items that come up on a regular basis.

Talented people want:

- To feel special and to be treated with respect.
- To have an atmosphere that's conducive to their productivity needs. This is a critical requirement, so HR functions and management must listen and act swiftly. Some of the current band of conditions seem to be:
  1. Free food and refreshments
  2. Break out and relaxation areas

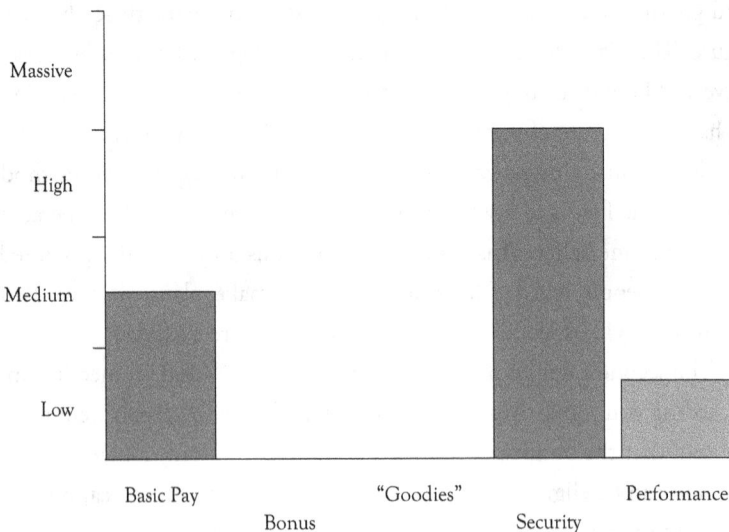

Figure 6.1 The worst output

3. Available pool cars

4. Flexible working hours and the option to work remotely if convenient.

5. Stock option scheme. For private companies, this has two significant benefits. Firstly, it gets buy-in and a feeling of ownership from the employee. Secondly, it is shown to reduce turnover if applied correctly.

6. In larger organizations, provision of services that help the individual, such as on-site medical facilities, complimentary laundry service, and child day care facilities.

7. To be led and guided, not managed and treated like a school kid.

8. A sense of purpose and direction.

The preceding figure is for your talented people, not poor performers. The trick is to *ask* talented people what they want (see Figure 6.2), then see if it can be provided. This is important if you want to retain your existing talent pool and attract new talent. Do not delegate this vital task to a nontalented person to organize.

Bonus is, of course, one of the most significant issues. We have discussed in an earlier chapter the productivity dashboard. In reality, a bonus will never be available to poor performers or a large percentage of the average performers. If you want a big bonus, you need to work for it.

Redirecting the bonus pot means it is now, now quite large. Your talented people can earn massive bonuses depending on how much value-added contribution they make to the organization (see Figure 6.3).

Old style employees	Talented employees
Likes to be managed	Likes leadership
Respect for the position	Respect for ability
Likes a job path	Likes career path
Promoted on time served	Promotion on ability
Needs rules	Common sense rules, just need guidelines
Unlikely to leave (often stuck in a rut)	C.V. Ready

Figure 6.2 The difference between old-type expectations and talented people's needs

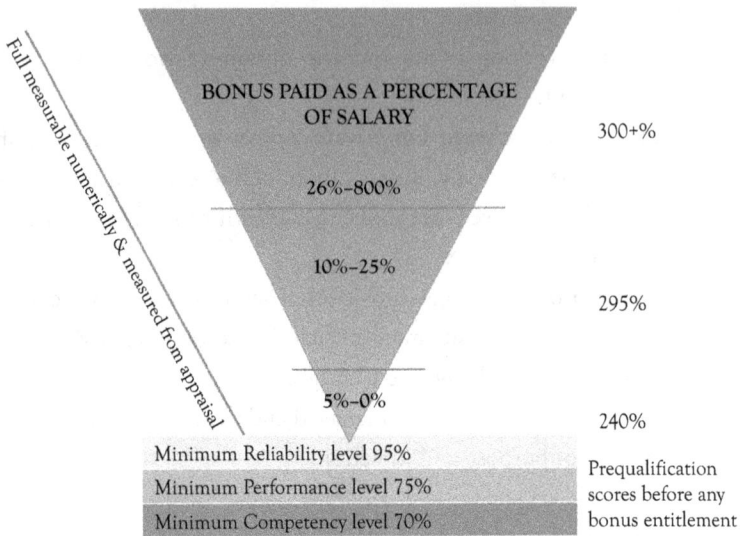

Figure 6.3 The bonus matrix—for talented people

The new approach is to pay employees for *what they do and contribute.* Not for their job title or what they know. This makes you wonder what the future holds for those companies that invest heavily in competency-based training. Do we want competent people, or are productivity and innovation the new key drivers?

In a large finance company in San Francisco, the highest paid person in the organization was a telesales agent, an exciting change in how we value and reward people.

Goodies

The giving of *goodies* for rewarding outstanding effort. Some companies have used this to good effect. In one company, the *gift* of a Land cruiser was offered and given to the manager who could reduce uncertificated sickness levels by the most significant percentage. Goodies are one-offs, not an entitlement or necessarily something that will be repeated regularly. The organization and the employee both benefit from the occasional use of goodies.

Innovation in goodies is critical, but it is imperative to find the right goodie, something that's really what the employees want. Some examples;

- A Caribbean holiday for the employee and family—all expenses paid for. The reward subject was "making the highest value ideas contribution to the organization."
- In the Middle East, for female employees, a female chauffeur-driven stretch limo—available on call for a year. This was in a bank call center where the employees were bringing in new business.

Excite and surprise! That is the key to good goodies that can make a difference.

Where Do Underperformers Fit?

In our new age of employment, underperformers need to sort themselves out. Training may help, but the root cause of many poor performers is that they are motivated by not working. Evidence is that they take up the most significant percentage of management time, account for the most training and in return, change is imperceivable. We have seen from our analysis earlier in the book that they are costly to employ and do very little work. In the *Ground Handling International Airport Magazine*, the suggested option for poor performers was to keep them off the premises until they could be released ultimately. While they are in the company, they add no value and often direct resources away from achieving critical organizational goals. You will see much evidence of this when the company is transitioning to take advantage of technology or when changing organizational shape. Poor performers are like a massive bolder blocking the stream of change. They need to be removed quickly.

Looking at the ratios of poor performers, average performers, and talented people, it is easy to see how to rebalance the organization after they have left. For sure, you will have fewer people in the organization. It will be surprising how much work can be done and how quickly things happen.

If we examine the way forward, the preferred option is to lose under-performers when rightsizing.

With the possibility of massive bonuses, goodies, and benefits for those who are talented, average performers have every incentive to do better. With inspirational leadership management, they will get help and encouragement, but, as we know from experience, ultimately, they have to change, and that choice is theirs alone. When examining underper-formers, it is a worthwhile exercise to find out who recruited them, and for what reason, they were deemed to be suitable.

Listen to Talented People

It is a skill good leader's already have. Talented people will come up with new ways of doing things and concepts that will cause a paradigm change; when they do, ensure you do not miss it.

Recruitment. Talented leaders are the only people who should do recruitment. The last thing you need is average people recruiting; you will end up with very average new personnel. All recruitment should involve testing and personality profiling. We have already discussed the impor-tance of personality profiling; testing is also essential as it tells us what the candidate can do now.

We know that internationally, there is widespread falsification of qual-ifications. This has been well reported in the HR press and international papers. One of the biggest and most widely reported was that of a doc-tor. He was employed in the UK and employed without any testing (see Figure 6.4). During his first week of out-of-hours home calls, he admin-istered a fatal dose of painkiller to one of his first patients and then fled the country to avoid prosecution. It transpired that he has a history of disastrous medical incidents. After a BBC investigation, it was found that it is likely he had never qualified as a medical doctor.

Some of the falsifications of CVs are so good that it would take private detective's months to check them out. Even if a fact on the CV is actual, like someone having a degree on a specific topic, there is always the issue of how fresh and up-to-date their knowledge is. We could examine CPE points, but do we have the time, and could we trust them?

Psychometric tests

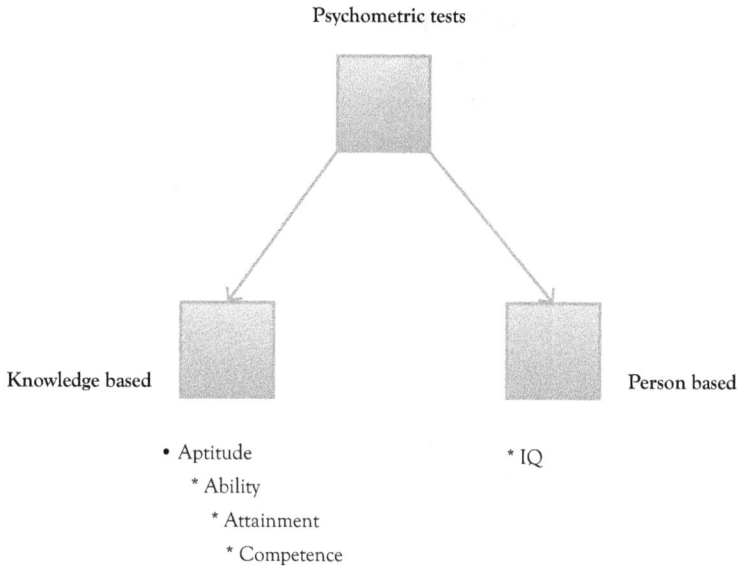

Knowledge based   Person based

• Aptitude   * IQ
* Ability
* Attainment
* Competence

Figure 6.4 Testing

What we are trying to establish with testing is: can the candidate do what we want them to do at the level they will be working and in their specialist area within our organization? This applies to all levels in the organization and for all but the most simple jobs.

About Testing and Its Development

Psychological tests are among our most powerful aids in the crucial problem of selecting and developing people at work. Estimates by some researchers have shown, for example, that significant increases in the GNP could result from the more widespread use of tests in selection. Testing shows us what someone can do today—it will show how the applicants compare not only to each other but also to an external benchmark referred to as a norm group. This can be formed either by occupation or by country data. Tests are now well established and a part of the business selection process. Most of the top performing world-leading companies use testing for selection recruitment and succession planning.

Tests are now used for all types and levels of job selection: from semi-skilled factory workers to senior management positions. Most of this usage tends to be in larger organizations, clearly not only because they employ more staff but also because they have more readily appreciated the difficulties of obtaining top-quality employees (talented employees).

What Is a Psychometric Test?

An occupational test is simply a psychological test used in the world of work. There have been numerous attempts to define what a psychological test is. One definition for a test is:

"A standardized sample of behavior which can be described by a numerical scale or category system" (Cronbach).

Psychological or *psychometric* tests aim to maximize objectivity by standardizing test conditions, instructions, time, content, scoring, and interpretation. All quality tests require that you (the tester) are qualified—this is enforced by the British Psychological Society and its American counterpart. Quality tests can only be purchased, administered, and interpreted by qualified staff only.

Psychometric tools can be divided into two broad categories: knowledge-based and person-based.

1. If we examine knowledge-based first—for our needs in recruitment work application, the tests measure ability, aptitude, attainment, and most importantly, competence. These tests conform to the same design principles, which are reliability, validity, standardization, and bias avoidance. The tests all have right or wrong answers, and the final score is often compared to a norm group. This ensures that you don't select based on the current test group but to the industry norm at the level, you are testing for. The *tests* run in strict examination conditions and are always timed. This applies to Web-based or pen/pencil face-to-face testing.

2. Person-based; the other form of testing is not widely used in industry and commerce but has a strong following with academics. These include IQ tests and others, which aim to measure general intelligence.

There are all sorts of tests you can use. The skill of the professional interviewer is to use only reliable tests that are valid for the job at hand.

Testing materials are best purchased from reputable suppliers, some of which are as follows:

- British Psychological Society
- American Psychological Society
- Saville and Holdsworth (SHL)
- The Test Agency—Hogrefe
- The Psychological Corporation

Recently, it has been widely accepted by psychologists that ability and personality profiling should be measured separately. There is no clear evidence that personality and ability are linked. As a result, testing is getting much more focused on work-related ability. Personality profilers have improved and focused entirely on personality and how this affects one's behavior in the workplace, despite their skills and abilities.

It is critical for good recruitment that branded tests are used, and I would advise using only materials from bona fide suppliers. The suppliers will have taken care to check that the validity and reliability trials all complied with the BPS and APS requirements and are fully defendable in case of litigation.

The interview should be particular, and each question should be scored simultaneously. A process approach to interviewing produces the most consistent, high-quality results (Miller 2017b).

This also applies to onboarding; the first few days with the company should be with talented people who inspire and can explain key company objectives.

Pay and rewards—balanced for success—the key issue.

We live in exciting times; keeping an open mind and taking chances is about the future. The speed of change is so fast that organizations need to be super agile to maximize the advantage change will bring. Remote working allows organizations to have globally based workforces so that *production* can operate 24 hours a day.

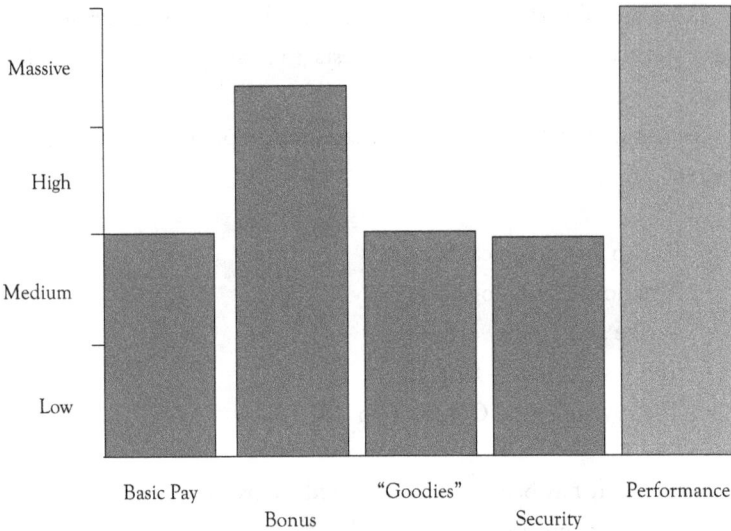

Figure 6.5 A system for winners

Just selecting one example of massive change, think of how electric vehicle power has changed the way we travel.

- 2022 the fastest growing sector in the automotive world— electric cars
- 2021 commercial air flights—electric
- 2022 autonomous taxis (no driver)
- 2023 Zoox robotaxi with supercar DNA rolls toward S.F., Vegas, Seattle streets
- Evia Aero, Germany, placed an order for 25 electric planes to be delivered in 2024

It is an example of one area of change and how it will affect the world now and in the future.

The Great Resignation

Talented people realize their value and, as such, are quick to change employers or just leave. It has been called the great resignation, and it is a global issue.

How to beat the great resignation? Some key points and insights from the Forbes article 2022:

1. Digital progress is accelerating. Science and technology continue to forge ahead in good markets and bad. Never bet against the rate of digital progress.
2. Anger at corporate tech tools. People under 40 worldwide are frustrated by the pace of digital transformation by *employers.*
3. Meaningful valuation differences create volatile talent flows. Smart employees—the kind you want at your company—see this. They want to work for tomorrow's winners.
4. The pandemic revealed that higher education is broken. It is increasingly overpriced for the value it delivers. The best employers will become educators.
5. The debate over return-to-office versus remote versus hybrid will not end soon. Each year, at-home and hybrid options become better. Do not pretend the optimal solution in mid-2022 will always be the best.
6. Mean bosses were not working so well before the pandemic. They do not work at all now.

Great companies will beat the great resignation.
—Rich Karlgaard Forbes, July 12, 2022

Differentiation—Is Needed Now!

The concept of differentiation is not new. It was introduced into General Electric by Jack Welch and first explained in detail in his bestselling book *Winning.* Jack Welch achieved much of his success at General Electric in America not just by using talent management techniques but by combining them with a firm and enforced differentiation policy. Other companies, too, have seen the benefits of differentiation but have come across three significant barriers.

Barriers to Differentiation

- Managers initially do not like it. The reason is that at the start of the process, it forces them to set and manage performance standards and to be accountable for the results. It also requires them to face poor performance in people and deal with it.

- HR managers who are more in line with the old-school personnel function do not understand. They still believe that their function is more welfare focused than productivity-focused and cannot be flexible enough to embrace such radical thinking—even if it does produce outstanding results.

- The final group is a sector of employees who can be best described as poor performers. These comprise what might be described as *the lazy, the mischievous, the dishonest and the incapable.* One whiff of any form of measurable productivity galvanizes this group into a unified block of employees whose mantras are "it won't work" and "it's unfair."

Differentiation sets out to divide your workforce into three distinct groups. The first of these is *talent.*

Talented people are found at all levels in the organization. The talent group, referred to as *movers,* as they tend to be mobile in their career aspirations, is the group that will form the basis for promotion, succession planning, leading change, and innovation. What is interesting about this group is that they make a difference in efficiency and bottom-line performance. As stated earlier, we know that the performance rating of these people is higher than that of average employees, at the moment, average employees tend to be the biggest group in most organizations.

It is essential rather than desirable that every effort is made to recruit, develop, and retain this group.

Talented people will move if there is not enough appreciation for the work that they do. This key point is why a differentiation policy is so important.

The second group—at present bulk of your workforce—are average employees. They do an adequate job. They are loyal and often stay with the company. This group is our *stickers.* They form the bulk of the organization and, as such, provide the stabilizing glue that keeps the organization together. There is no reason why some people in this group, regardless of service length with the company or their age, cannot up their game and move into the talented group.

The final group is poor performers. These are people whom you need to move out of the organization. They consist of people who are a product of poor recruitment, often recruited in haste or by people whose only recruitment criterion was "I like them."

The *lazy* are also in this group. They are really organizational thieves who take the organization's money but do not do the work. The final collection here seems to be for those who are dissatisfied. Typically, they are constantly complaining and spreading dissatisfaction. They blame everyone except themselves. Anyone in HR could list the names of the people in this group. They usually have massive HR files and are well known in the organization. Use some sound advice from Jeff Bezos.

I'd rather interview 50 people and not hire anyone than hire the wrong person.

Jeff Bezos–Amazon

The struggle many talented people have is the lack of differentiation in old-style organizations. Most of the organizational focus seems to be on poor performers, rules, and regulations written for the same group. This is particularly evident in the public sector and older-style organizations. The problem is often compounded by HR functions that focus on being *fair* to everyone rather than doing the best for the organization they serve.

In Chapter 2, we calculated the cost of poor performers and also found that they were a group who were motivated by not working. We could also see how different the three groups were, talented people, average people, and poor performers. With this information, even the public sector is in a position to argue the case for differentiation in:

- Pay
- Training
- Bonus and reward systems
- How employee benefits are allocated

The way forward, as we have already discussed, is to pay people for what they *do*, not their job title, years in the organization or the fact they tick all the boxes for being competent. If you are going to create a for-ward-focused organization and an organization that is a place for talented people to excel, then differentiation is needed, even if it seems at first to be rather draconian.

A *Cautionary Note*

Talented people can be in any age group—X, Y, or Z. Generation Z are often misquoted as troublesome millennials. A correct definition is Generation Z, also referred to as iGen; they are a group of bright, often experienced—less individuals who believe they are *entitled*—entitled to everything, promotion, not questioned, higher salary, maximum bonus. The list goes on; some may be talented, the majority are just tricky, and most not very socially aware. This group is not a unit of 100 percent talented people—so be careful. Old-style managers are quick to point out their shortcomings and incorrectly label them as troublesome and impossible to work with.

CHAPTER 7

The Use of Behavioral Economics to Get Results

Understanding Behavioral Economics and the Role of Applied Psychology

The role or definition of behavioral economics is complex. It has been made so as the topic seems to have been hijacked by academics who have made the entire issue unnecessarily overcomplicated and jargon bound. In this short section of the book, we will focus on how to get the best from psychology-based activities, which will add value to your organization.

Our first case study example will look at a call center. This call center specializes in providing car insurance for affinity groups. Sales had reached a plateau, and a solution was needed to increase sales—specifically at the renewal point.

A significant proportion of the customers were government employees—so they were very rule-following and conservative in their actions and thinking. The agents dealing with the customers were, in the main young, rather extrovert, and outspoken.

After an analysis of the way, the agents spoke and with a profile of the customers. Call center agents' scripts were changed to be more in line with the customers. The customers were very procedure-based. The scripts reflected this using procedural language such as:

- The next step will be … .
- You will then get the documentation in five days; then, you can pay the balance.
- The process for renewal is in two steps—first, you make a payment … .

The outcome of this simple change was an almost immediate increase in sales and retention. The economics were driven by a shift in behavior and a simple piece of psychology.

People like people like themselves.

It's referred to as homophily, the tendency to associate with similar others, and is a fundamental pattern underlying human relationships.

This type of thinking is the basis of neuro linguistic programs (NLPs), which is worth investigating as it will enhance your communication skills both written and spoken. You will be able to find out all you need by reading one of the many books on this topic. Communication is one of our six leadership skills—Chapter 1.

Leadership skill 4. Great leaders recognize that communication takes time, and that you can't correct the past.

Political leaders often use emotional worlds that change beliefs to meet often hidden agendas.

In the recent conflict in the Ukraine, words like *our friends* were used to gain public support, boosted later by the comment "The Russians may have chemical weapons and could use Nuclear weapons." All are playing on the fact—we help our friends, we don't abandon them.

Many of you will recall, in the UK, the endless talk about Iraq having weapons of mass destruction to galvanize popular opinion ready for war. After the dust settled—where were these weapons?

Playing on people's emotions and beliefs was a contributing factor to Donald Trump becoming the president of the United States. Most of that information was gathered from information purchased on people's behavior and their predominant personality profile. If you think this does not work, Donald Trump became the president. Applying basic psychology and behavioral information can be a potent tool.

The IBM Watson tool is very good at analyzing language patterns, both written and spoken. We can then get a much better understanding of individuals or groups of people and use that information perhaps to our economic advantage.

Behavioral Economics and Its Link to Individuals and Success

Instilling a *can do* culture to maximize productivity and reduce turnover is nothing without a clear, consistent, and well-understood approach. The objective is to develop existing people and create talented people. An example you would appreciate from this book is identifying potential talented people from your top average employees and providing they meet the criteria and are willing. You are providing that group with an opportunity to excel. Crossing that barrier is a big one. With a group development program, it can be done by making sure success at every stage is recognized and applauded. This is behavioral psychology in action. If 50 percent were successful, it would send a powerful message to others in the average group to try harder. As success breeds success, the successful group's progress must be monitored and reported via the company communications system at every opportunity. What you are then doing by design is *nudging* others to try harder, even if they don't join the talented group. Where does the economics fit? The real beneficiary will be the company, getting greater productivity without recruiting and raising productivity levels in the organization. As you create a cohort of inspirational leaders and change the management style, the balance of how the organization works will change.

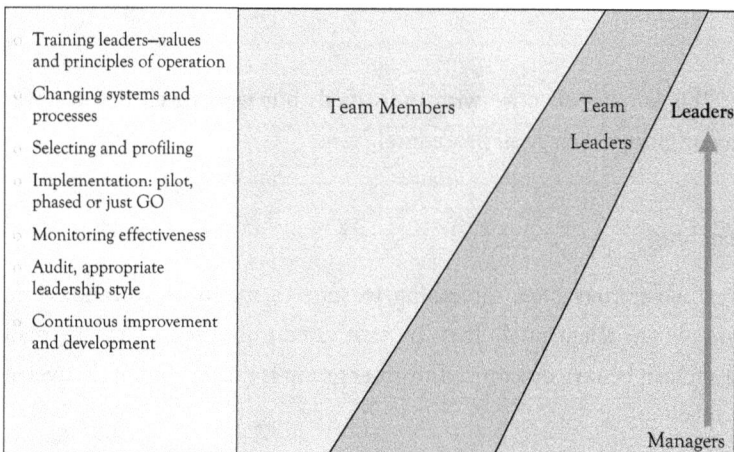

Figure 7.1 The process of change—how we change our organization

The nudge theory is helpful to remember; it is a concept in behavioral economics, political theory, and behavioral sciences that proposes positive reinforcement and indirect suggestions as ways to influence the behavior and decision making of groups or individuals.

Source: Wikipedia.

AI and nudging, a piece in the *Harvard Business Review* published in 2021 was one of the first articles to coin the term *algorithmic nudging*.

"Companies are increasingly using algorithms to manage and control individuals not by force, but rather by nudging them into desirable behaviour — in other words, learning from their personalized data and altering their choices in some subtle way." Nudging is a very successful way of getting things done like a drip feed.

Earlier in this chapter, we mentioned using NLP, neuro linguistic programming, helps us understand the certain types. This gives a much better understanding of how best to deliver information to the team.

The three types are

1. People who prefer *options* to make a decision. People who prefer *procedures* to make decisions.
2. *Away from*–influenced by avoiding troubles or difficulties. *Toward*— just like to see results—oblivious often to the problems.
3. *Internals* like to make the decision, not that worried about what others are doing. *Externals* like to know what others are doing and will often say, "what's the majority of people doing/ thinking about this?"

This is most effective with individuals but works well if you have a similar group, such as all procedural.

Coaching

Even self-starters need something to start them. In organizations, this group is our talent pool. They are motivated once their minds are made up and can be very dynamic. The other group is the top end of the average people.

Power coaching is not necessarily a pleasant process. It aims to push people for measurable improvement over a fixed period. This is very like the approach a team captain would take. Two documents are necessary. The first is a record of the coaching advice. This record keeps track of the benchmark at the beginning of the coaching phase and then tracks performance every two weeks for a maximum of 14 weeks. The second document is a performance chart that shows the charted performance increase over a period of time. This chart is an excellent motivator for the person being coached as they can see their incremental performance improvement.

This system really works. Here are some examples from three very different companies, UK and United States:

Financial services—20 percent improvement in sales

Insurance group—50 percent improvement in competence

Financial holdings—30 percent improvement in sales

The coaching sessions are typically 20 to 30 minutes long, sometimes less. The coach needs to be someone who will push for improvement, usually the leader.

Understanding the Vital Role of Profiling and OCEAN

If you are looking for potential leaders, remote workers, finance personnel, creative people, change managers, and innovators, then profiling is critical to making the right decision. The psychology of profiling will produce much better decisions on job selection and, in particular, stop the organization from allowing just anyone to become a home worker. For home workers to be successful, you will need people with the correct profile, or you will have a disaster on your hands very quickly. The old-style managers will then be quick to say, "I told you so. I said it would never work."

Examine the profile of high-performing and diligent remote workers—that will be a good step in providing a tailored template for your organization. In an earlier chapter, a reasonable template is available as a start.

OCEAN should be used for all new entrants into the organization as a norm and when selecting personnel for promotion. Personality will give you the employee fit; testing will show you if they have the capability.

Organizational Change

With change being the biggest organizational issue, you should also examine creating a corporate culture template.

How does it work? You can purchase such prewritten templates from companies like SHL, or you can get one crafted for your organization. Why reinvent the wheel?

A typical template covers four crucial areas

1. Performance
2. Human resources
3. Decision making
4. Relationships

Each of the key areas is subdivided; in the case of performance, it is split into six areas (see Figure 7.2).

STAGE 1. The first step in the process is to gather a group of people; we call them the visionaries.

This group are those that have a strong view of how the organization will need to be in the future. It's important that this group are the real visionaries, not the management team by title.

The group attended a briefing that explained that the future normally requires a different culture or is equipped to handle new ways of working to make the organization successful.

Each topic is explained, after which the team (at the exact same time) raise a card that gives the value of the topic 1 through 10. *The 10 cards are provided to each of the attendees.*

At the end of the exercise, a template is constructed, showing where the organization needs to be in the future.

1. Performance–SHL model

1	2	3	4	5	6	7	8	9	10	
		O					X			Concern for quantity 1.1
						X/O				Concern for quality 1.2
					O	X				Use of new equipment 1.3
			X/O							Encouragement of creativity 1.4
				O			X			Customer orientation 1.5
				O			X			Commercial orientation 1.6

O = Current   X = Goal

Figure 7.2 Where we want to be versus where we are now

STAGE 2. Every staff member is given the questionnaire about corporate culture; this is done in a room and completed by each delegate individually; no names are on the form as you want honest answers.

Later, when that is done, the averages are worked out and written on your visionaries template.

On the chart, the visionary's requirement of the future is shown as an *X,* and the employee's understanding of the present is shown as an *O.*

STAGE 3. The second workshop of the visionaries (2 to 3 hours)

The average score is marked on a template and only available to the visionaries. Where it is revealed and is at the visionary's second briefing. As you can see in Figure 7.2, it's not even a close match. For each main heading, performance, for example, the visionaries need to decide what's critical to change—you can't change everything in one go. This is another case of where nudging will take place.

> *Changing the culture takes time; it needs to be controlled very carefully. Most change requires nudging and a constant and consistent approach.*

The first heading is Performance. The group will discuss which template topics need to be altered to get the desired culture for the future. In our example, the most pressing were:

Concern for quantity 1.1. In the business, this was a significant concern as the marketplace had changed, and profit margins were suddenly reduced. The need to do more was the big issue, and a series of interventions was needed to nudge employees into believing they needed to do a lot more to be competitive.

Customer orientation 1.5. This was the second area for attention; the media to do this over time to publish in the company monthly news bulletin competitor comparison facts and the need to retain customers. The visionary group agreed that this and the drive to do more would automatically raise the commercial orientation in the organization, shown as 1.6 on the chart.

It was agreed that the task would be split between various visionaries in the group, and SAPs would be produced for 1.1 concern for quantity and 1.5 customer orientation; this would be reviewed and agreed upon at a future meeting.

And so, the culture change was to start, based on a template, what the visionaries' need for the future—where we need to go. Then the reality check, what do the employees think now? All that was left was to design several direct interventions and have a series of nudges to move the culture to the desired position to achieve organizational success. It sounds simple but takes time and a very steady and universal series of nudges.

The nudging approach in behavioral economics is a very subtle way of getting things done without causing too many waves in the organization.

Getting results from corporate culture change take time; survey no more than twice a year and be very quiet in the way you do it.

Change

Throughout this book, we have looked at how AI, the effects of COVID-19, remote working, and robotics will change the world of work forever. So, it's a challenging period for the organization because these three strategies tend to occur simultaneously.

We are dealing with system issues; we are trying to extend the organization as it is, and somebody's probably trying to transition or redefine the organization.

It's a tough time; morale at the moment could become an issue; it's extremely hard on people, particularly those with a personality profile low O.

The most natural thing organizations do is to try to extend out what they are already doing. This is not the answer, change is here right now, and it will be the most significant paradigm shift since the Industrial Revolution.

In the short term, some organizations may restructure; they tend to extend their efficiency by cutting costs and cutting people. As a result of cutting costs and cutting people, you'll often hear the organization talks about having to work harder rather than be different.

We are seeing many organizations selling off marginal businesses at this point as a way to raise cash. These methodologies are patches. What's needed is a fundamental change in line with the massive paradigm shift that's taking place.

The key issues needing addressing right now are:

- Leaders, not managers, use the new skillset.
- Benefit from remote working but profile remote workers first.
- Think differently, rightsize.
- Produce a culture for your future needs.
- Get rid of poor performers—your organization can't afford them.
- Embrace AI and ChatGPT—don't waste time fighting it.
- Rewrite employee handbooks—write for talented performers, guidelines only.
- Have new contracts of employment—fashioned by legal specialists.
- Introduce bonus systems that inspire talented people.
- *Listen* to talented people.
- Provide talented people with an environment that is conducive to their high performance.
- Uses performance appraisal as a motivational tool—look to the future.
- *The future is bright—but only for those leaders who seize the opportunity.*

Bibliography

Benefits From Home Are Working Very Successful in the First Year but Hard to Maintain. 2021. World News, World Economic Forum.

Bezos, J. 2021. *35 Jeff Bezos Quotes on Leadership.* Market me good.

Buffett, W. 2020. *23 Quotes on Leadership and Success.* Quotes for Entrepreneurs.

Calder, S. 2022. "Rail Travel in the U.K." *The Independent Newspaper.*

Clark, M. 2023. "Home Worker Ordered to Repay Employer $2,756." *New York Independent Newspaper.*

Costa, P. and R. McCrae. 1999. "Five-Factor Theory of Personality." In *Handbook of Personality; Theory and Research*, pp. 139–153, 2nd ed. New York, NY: Guildford.

Courtis, J. n.d. *Managing by Mistake.* Paperback book. Institute of Chartered Accountants.

Daoanis, L. 2012. *Performance Appraisal Systems: Its Implication to Employee Performance.*

Dé, R. and R. Tripathi. 2020. *Homeworker Pay Would Need to Be Revisited. Paying People for What They Do Rather Than for Their Position and What They Know.* Published paper.

Forsdick, S. June 12, 2022. "A.I. Synthetic Data Bias-Free." *The Time's Newspaper.*

Furnham, A. 2000. *MAD SAD and BAD Management.* Management Books.

Furnham, A. 2010. *The Elephant in the Board Room.* Palgrave McMillan.

Hanssen, L. 2022. *Research on Commuter Travel Costs.* Researcher.

Ihsan, Z. and A. Furnham. 2018. *The New Technologies in Personality Assessment.*

Kelly, J. 2022. *Instead of Hybrid, Remote or In-Office Work Styles, This May Be A Better Option.*

Kosinski, M. 2017. *The End of Privacy Keynote Speech.* Stanford, CA: Stanford.

Kosinski, M. 2021. "Facial Recognition Technology Can Expose Political Orientation From Naturalistic Facial Images." *Journal Scientific Reports* 11, pp. 1–7.

Kucera, T. 2021. *Owls, Larks, and Productivity.* The G Leader.

Laricchia, F. 2022. *Global Apple Mac Sales 2021.* Statista.

LHH. 2022. "The War on Talent Is Won by Investing in Peoples Careers." *Sunday Times.*

Lim, A.G. 2020. *N.E.O. Definitions.* Simple Psychology.

Miller, T. 2010. *Understanding and Measuring Competence and Performance.* Google Scholar.

Miller, T. 2017a. *H.R. Analytics and Innovations in Workforce Planning.* New York, NY: Business Expert Press.

Miller, T. 2017b. *Successful Interviewing—A Talent-Focused Approach to Successful Recruitment and Selection.* New York, NY: Business Expert Press.

Miller, T. 2021. "Useful Formula and the Productivity Dashboard." *A.I. and Remote Working,* Ch. 5. New York, NY: Business Expert Press.

Miller, T. 2022. *A.I. and Remote Working—The End of H.R.* Google Scholar.

Miller, T. and W. Best. 2020. *Leadership Style Questionnaire.*

Miller, T. and G. Mack. 2021. *The Global Changing World of Work.* YouTube Interview.

Miller, T. and G. Mack. 2021. *How to Rightsize Your Organization.* YouTube interview.

Miller, T. n.d.-a. *Innovations in Workforce Planning,* pp. 44–60. New York, NY: Business Expert Press.

Miller, T. n.d.-b. *Recruitment and Selection.* New York, NY: Business Expert Press.

Mok, A. and J. Zinkula. 2023. *Employment at Risk.* Business insider.

Musk, E. 2022. *49 Quotes.* Wealthy Celebrity quote 12.

Nierenberg, R. 2017. *The Music Paradigm.* BBC The Money Program.

Parker, K., J. Horowitz, and R. Minkin. 2022. *COVID-19 Pandemic Continues To Reshape Work in America.* P.E.W. Research Centre.

Robinson, B. 2022a. *Effectiveness of Hybrid and Remote Work.* Forbes.

Robinson, B. 2022b. *New Study on Remote Work and Happiness.* Forbes.

Sachs, G. March 2023. "The Jobs Most at Risk From AI Automation." *Apple News.*

Sanchez, D.G., N.G. Parra, C. Ozden, B. Rijkers, M. Viollaz, and H. Winkler. 2020. *Globally One in Five Jobs Can Be Done From Home, Less in Underdeveloped Countries.* Published research paper.

Seymour, S. 2022. *Work From Home Productivity Studies.* Finances Online.

Sherman, R. 2019a. "Beware These Marketing Trends in Psychological Assessment and Why You Shouldn't Fall for Them." *Psychology Today.*

Sherman, R. October 17, 2019b. "Beware These Marketing Trends in Psychological Assessment and Why You Shouldn't Fall for Them." *Psychology Today.*

Sinek, S. 2016. *Millennials in the Workplace.* I.Q. Interview.

Sutton, R. and B. Wigert. 2019. *More Harm Than Good: The Truth About Performance Reviews.* Workplace.

The Harris Pole. 2023. "Skill Workers Most Fear Chat GPT Will Replace." *Fortune Magazine.*

Thiel, P. and B. Masters. 2014. "Startups and Building the Future." *Zero to One.*

Tsipursky, G. 2023. *76% of Managers Now Agree—Hybrid Employees Are More Productive.* Entrepreneur.

Welch, J. 2005. *Winning.* Harper Collins.

Welch, J. 2019. "Rank and Yank. That Is Not How It's Done." *Wall Street Journal.*

Whitworth, D. 2021. *About A.I.* Times Magazine interview.

Wolfer, S. 2022. "9 Best Benefits of Working From Home." *The Muse—Work-Life Balance.*

www.youtube.com/watch?v=J6VTbIRU4ls.

www.youtube.com/watch?v=vYFgc-KZhnQ.

Zuckerburg, M. 2022. *30 Best Quotations.* Bloggersideas. quote 29.

About the Author

Dr. Tony Miller, MBA, FCIPD, FinstAM, MRSH, MAPS, MBPS, FILM, is an Occupational Psychologist Consultant who specializes in improvements through people using new leadership techniques and change with artificial intelligence (AI), rightsizing, and remote working. In the past few years, he has had published 33 books, one of which is in Chinese, and also 10 audio books. Well-traveled, he has worked worldwide in 36 countries in the past 10 years, including the United States, and has acted as a specialist consultant for some of the world's most prestigious companies. His ability to continually create outstanding performance through people has resulted in his appearing on TV regularly. Recently he designed a mathematical model to enable any organization to calculate precisely how many people it needs, essential for any implementation of ChatGPT, AI, and remote working applications. He is much sought-after as a speaker and runs masterclasses and management briefings on creating organizational improvement and changing managers into dynamic leaders, suited to the new paradigm in our world of work.

An interview about this book is available to see on YouTube www.youtube.com/watch?v=LNLUf6QTBMg.

Index

OTHER TITLES IN THE HUMAN RESOURCE MANAGEMENT AND ORGANIZATIONAL BEHAVIOR COLLECTION

Michael J. Provitera, Barry University, Editor

- *11 Secrets of Nonprofit Excellence* by Kathleen Stauffer
- *The Nonprofit Imagineers* by Ben Vorspan
- *At Home With Work* by Nyla Naseer
- *Improv to Improve Your Leadership Team* by Candy Campbell
- *Leadership In Disruptive Times* by Sattar Bawany
- *The Intrapreneurship Formula* by Sandra Lam
- *Navigating Conflict* by Lynne Curry
- *Innovation Soup* by Sanjay Puligadda and Don Waisanen
- *The Aperture for Modern CEOs* by Sylvana Storey
- *The Future of Human Resources* by Tim Baker
- *Change Fatigue Revisited* by Richard Dool and Tahsin I. Alam
- *Championing the Cause of Leadership* by Ted Meyer
- *Embracing Ambiguity* by Michael Edmondson
- *Breaking the Proactive Paradox* by Tim Baker
- *The Modern Trusted Advisor* by Nancy MacKay and Alan Weiss

Concise and Applied Business Books

The Collection listed above is one of 30 business subject collections that Business Expert Press has grown to make BEP a premiere publisher of print and digital books. Our concise and applied books are for…

- Professionals and Practitioners
- Faculty who adopt our books for courses
- Librarians who know that BEP's Digital Libraries are a unique way to offer students ebooks to download, not restricted with any digital rights management
- Executive Training Course Leaders
- Business Seminar Organizers

Business Expert Press books are for anyone who needs to dig deeper on business ideas, goals, and solutions to everyday problems. Whether one print book, one ebook, or buying a digital library of 110 ebooks, we remain the affordable and smart way to be business smart. For more information, please visit www.businessexpertpress.com, or contact sales@businessexpertpress.com.

www.ingramcontent.com/pod-product-compliance
Lightning Source LLC
Chambersburg PA
CBHW061327220326

41599CB00026B/5067